HAVING THE

#1

REPUTATION

GLOBAL
PUBLISHING
G R O U P

Global Publishing Group
Australia • New Zealand • Singapore • America • London

I0035866

HAVING THE #1 REPUTATION

REPUTATION

How to Master
The Greatest Asset
in Leadership and Business

DARRELL HARDIDGE

First Edition 2025

National Library of Australia
Cataloguing-in-Publication entry:

Having the #1Reputation: How to Master The Greatest Asset in Leadership and Business - Darrell Hardidge

1st ed.
ISBN 978-1-925370-48-5 (pbk.)
ISBN 978-1-925370-49-2 (ebook)

A catalogue record for this book is available from the National Library of Australia
NATIONAL LIBRARY OF AUSTRALIA

Published by Global Publishing Group
PO Box 258, Banyo, QLD 4014 Australia
Email admin@globalpublishinggroup.com.au

For further information about orders:
Phone: +61 7 3267 0747

Dedication

To the true leaders—those who understand that **excellence is a pursuit, not a destination**. You know your greatest achievements are never built alone, but made possible by the unwavering support of others.

To the champions of business—**from the front line to the boardroom**—who recognise that greatness is only realised through the power of alignment. You lead teams who share a vision far greater than the demands of today.

To those who live by the truth that **until you serve a purpose greater than yourself, you will never rise beyond yourself**. Leadership, at its core, is the ability to empower others to do what they never thought possible.

To those just beginning the journey—**everything you need is within reach**. But first, you must show that you can be trusted to hold the chalice of responsibility, and carry it with honour.

Greatness isn't given. It's earned. And it awaits.

Acknowledgments

This book has been a challenge, especially when creating a completely new model that makes others obsolete. It has tested the status quo of what most believe to be the ultimate objective—**customer satisfaction**, the average of averages. But to measure a #1Reputation—the best of the best—requires a new way of thinking and a bold new protocol to define it. It took over 15 years to discover and tens of thousands of perfect 10/10 experiences to shape. Thinking outside the box is one thing—**operating** outside of it is something else entirely.

None of this would have been possible without an extraordinary leadership team. **Alice, Maria, Elle, and Denise**—your combined 56 years of unwavering commitment to Saguity have delivered standards of brilliance that have made this new model possible. Thank you for your dedication, loyalty, and professionalism.

To the incomparable **Marshall Thurber and Bill Allen**—without your original support, wisdom, and training, these discoveries would have never been made. You're in our thoughts every day. Every new company we work with learns your names and benefits from your influence.

To **Michael Stillwell**, this is the third book where you've generously given your time, insight, and guidance. Your counsel is deeply appreciated, and your input is woven through every chapter. Thank you once again, you are a true champion of business.

To the thousands of **extraordinary people** I've had the privilege of working with in workshops and keynotes—you make every session unique, impactful, and fun. You remind me every day why this work matters.

And to our incredible **clients**, who place deep trust in our process—we're forever grateful for your partnership. We will never stop improving for you. **Together, we're better.**

#1REPUTATION
YOUR GREATEST ASSET

Contents

Introduction

The Hidden Asset That Builds Empires or Burns Them Down

There's an asset in your business more powerful than revenue, product, or people.

It decides who will buy from you, work for you, refer you, partner with you—or walk away without a word.

It opens doors in seconds or slams them shut for years.

It's your **reputation**.

And if you're not consciously building it, you're already at risk.

Your **personal, professional, and company reputation** is not just a line item in goodwill. It's the **unseen force** driving every opportunity—or blocking them. It's the single greatest leverage point in any leadership role. And yet ... most executives never talk about it. Most don't know how to measure it, and almost none have a structured plan to **protect and scale** it.

That's what this book is about.

It's not theory. It's not branding fluff. It's the practical blueprint built from over **500,000 phone-based interviews** with high-value customers in complex B2B and B2C markets. This is the truth behind what the market *really thinks*—not what your team says, your NPS email tells you, or your gut wants to believe.

Let me ask you:

- Who, exactly, is responsible for your company's reputation?

- Who decides what your reputation is and who controls it?

- When was the last time your executive team had a strategic discussion about measuring it and protecting it?

- How do your team, your suppliers, and your customers define your reputation—*and are they aligned?*

- What systems are in place to detect reputation risk *before* it costs you clients, cash, or culture?

You think you'd know if something was wrong, right?

Wrong. That's the trap. It's called **the Great Assumption**—the belief that if revenue is strong and complaints are low, everything must be fine.

It's not. Because reputation isn't measured by internal opinion. It's decided by the **market**—and the market isn't giving you a second chance.

Reputation is alive. It evolves every day. It precedes your pitch, influences every deal, and decides how much margin you can hold. It's either compounding value, or silently bleeding it.

And right now, it's either working *for* you—or *against* you.

Over 16 years of customer experience (CX) research, I've worked with market leaders like BMW, STIHL, Coates Hire, APT, Honda, Karndean, Pronto Software, Ektimo, Macsteel, GJ Gardner Homes, and hundreds of ambitious companies who punched above their weight in competitive industries. The common thread wasn't marketing spend or operational structure—it was leadership clarity around one thing:

Reputation is not a marketing function. It's a leadership strategy.

It's the true north that guides decision-making, drives loyalty, attracts talent, commands trust, and builds legacies.

Great leaders measure and manage their reputation like any other strategic asset. The average ones ignore it until it's too late—until the customer leaves, the employee resigns, the market shifts, or the negative perception snowballs into a cultural cancer.

This book will show you how to **design, measure, and scale** a #1 Reputation (#1R). Not just customer satisfaction—**customer appreciation**. Not just employee engagement—**team advocacy**. Not just supplier relationships—**strategic alliances**.

You'll learn how to build reputation across four critical leverage zones:

1. **Employer of Choice** – Where culture becomes your competitive moat.

2. **Customer Excellence** – Where appreciation replaces satisfaction and drives lifetime loyalty.

3. **Supplier Relations** – Where you become the #1 customer and gain speed, access, and margin.

4. **Owner & Investor Confidence** – Where belief in the mission drives long-term risk-taking and value creation.

Inside these pages is the strategic reputation playbook you were never taught in MBA school or executive briefings.

You'll discover:

- How to transform reputation into a measurable, defensible asset

- The silent killers of reputation hiding in your business right now

- The fatal mistake of using customer satisfaction as your benchmark

- Why internal opinions mean nothing—and how to replace them with data that predicts risk

- How to lead a culture that becomes the most trusted name in your industry

- How to operationalise reputation into every process—from CX to account management to executive reporting

Your reputation is always in motion. It's either working for you, expanding your influence and earning you compound trust …

Or it's quietly eroding, waiting to be exposed when you can least afford it.

This book is your line in the sand.

Because the companies that dominate the next decade won't just have the best products or services.

They'll be the #**1 most trusted**.

How to Use This Book

#1Reputation is not a storybook you need to follow from beginning to end. It's a strategy manual. A blueprint. A challenge.

You can read it front to back, and I hope you do—but you don't have to. Some chapters will hit home more than others depending on your role, your goals, or the challenges you're facing right now. Use it as a toolkit. Jump to the parts that matter most. Share chapters with your team. Pin pages to your strategy meetings. Use the insights to provoke conversation, challenge assumptions, and spark transformation.

This book was built for **leaders who roll up their sleeves**. If you're looking for inspiration, it's here—but more importantly, so is **implementation**.

You might need to pause between chapters to apply something you've just read. That's exactly how it's meant to work. The goal isn't to finish it. The goal is to **use it**.

The only thing I ask of you is this:
Don't keep the knowledge to yourself.

Use it to build momentum, align your people, and elevate your culture. Share it. Debate it. Challenge the status quo. Because if you do that, you'll uncover one of the most powerful levers in business—**the #1 Reputation advantage**.

Let's get to work.

CHAPTER 1

GREATNESS AWAITS

#1

CHAPTER 1
GREATNESS AWAITS

Who are you not to be great?

You—yes, you—with the imagination to see opportunities that no one else can yet see. You, who dares to envision a future others don't yet understand.
You, with the courage to stand apart, not to conform, not to shrink back, but to build something remarkable.

Who are you to settle for ordinary when you were born with the capacity for the extraordinary?

You are not here to be a cog in someone else's machine. You are here to carve your own path, to design a future that only you can define. You have the power to rewrite your story with a single phrase: **"I Am."** Those two words hold the power to shift your identity, reshape your mindset, and relaunch your life into a future you imagine.

So, ask yourself: Who are you to remain anonymous, to sit silently in the shadows, to deny your own brilliance?

Because when you deny it to yourself, you deny the whole world.

Greatness Awaits.

You Are the Architect of Your Reputation

You get to decide what your reputation becomes. Will you build a legacy of integrity, growth, and value? Or will you remain passive—conforming, shrinking, hoping for change while doing little to create it?

Your **personal and professional reputation** is one of your greatest assets. In your career, it's your golden chalice—an invisible force that either unlocks doors or closes them.

The most powerful reputations are forged through integrity and service, not ego and manipulation. Every interaction matters. Every action adds or subtracts from the account of trust others hold in you.

If you build your reputation by adding value to others, you'll be rewarded with opportunity, respect, and a career of limitless expansion. But if your gains come at the expense of others, the cost will always catch up with you. There will be challenges. Maybe controversy. Maybe criticism. But you are never powerless. You can always choose who you want to be known as. And when you choose to rebuild with responsibility, honesty, character, and consistency—**greatness reclaims its place**.

Make Your Career Matter

You will likely spend the next 10, 20, 30 years in your chosen career path. That time will shape your identity, your lifestyle, and your legacy. So, make it count.

From the first moment you entered your professional journey, you began laying the foundation of your reputation. But ask yourself:

- Did I build it like an engineer—structured, strong, and guided by clear principles?

- Did I design it like an architect—creative, visionary, and inspiring?

- Or did I leave it to chance—drifting without intention, while building someone else's dream instead of my own?

Regardless of how your past looks, here's the good news: **Your future is not set in stone**.

You can carve out a new direction. You can elevate the one you've built. You can secure it, shape it, and scale it. A powerful reputation can take you on a journey of discovery and abundance—and it starts with a decision.

Greatness Awaits.

This Book Is for Everyone

This book isn't just for executives, business owners, or industry leaders. It's for anyone, in any role, who wants to build something meaningful and leave a mark in their world.

Because building a powerful reputation isn't about self-promotion. It's about contribution.

It's about creating a vision bigger than yourself.

"Until you have a purpose bigger than yourself, you cannot go beyond yourself"

Dr John Demartini

A reputation built on ego eventually collapses. A reputation built on service creates sustainability. It becomes your invitation to higher levels of opportunity, growth, and influence.

You will always rise to your next level of incompetence—and what you choose to do at that level determines what's next. Will you embrace the growth? Or retreat to comfort?

Everything you do impacts the reputation your identity is built on, and the more value you add to yourself, the more value you can give to others. That's the multiplier of success. The greater your professional reputation, the more doors that open—and the more power you have to choose which ones to walk through.

The Seven Life Arenas of a #1Reputation

Think of the most respected people you know—the ones with what we call a **#1 Reputation (#1R)**. You'll find them in one or more of these seven life arenas:

1. **Family**

2. **Social**

3. **Financial**

4. **Vocation**

5. **Spiritual**

6. **Physical**

7. **Mental**

Some are strong in a few areas, others in just one—but what matters most is the **principles** they follow.

Those with powerful reputations live by foundational values:

- **Integrity**: They do what they say they'll do

- **Responsibility**: They step up and take ownership—no blame, no excuses

- **Growth Mindset**: They seek to learn, adapt, and discover what they don't yet know

- **Contribution**: They believe in adding value, not extracting it

These people don't chase status. They build substance—and status follows.

Reputation: A Cautionary Tale

Many people race to build their reputation quickly—to climb fast, to get noticed. And that's understandable. The faster you rise the sooner you access bigger opportunities. But beware: reputation built without integrity is a house of cards.

The higher you go, the more structure you need to protect your reputation. One misstep, and the fall can be swift and severe.

We've seen it too often—public figures whose reputations are damaged or destroyed, sometimes in a single day. Why? Because ego clouded their judgment. They didn't see the cost of their actions—or believed they were immune to consequence.

Think about Tiger Woods. In a single moment, his off-course decisions impacted his on-course legacy. Why? Because reputation is holistic. It's not compartmentalised. People don't separate your character from your career.

Reputation amplifies everything. Protect it at all costs.

Design Your #1R Strategy

You don't need to wait for luck or title. You can start designing your #1R today—deliberately, intelligently, and authentically.

Here's how:

1. Find the Mentors

Seek out those who already have a #1R in the area you aspire to grow in. Use platforms like LinkedIn or, even better, secure a personal referral.

2. Reach Out with Purpose

Ask to meet them—in person or via video—and humbly request their insights. Let them know you're on a journey and would value their wisdom and experience.

3. Ask the Right Questions

Design thoughtful questions. Try:

"If you had to start again, what would you do differently?"
"What were the most powerful actions you took to build your reputation?"

"Who did you look up to for guidance when building your reputation?"

4. Interview Ten People

Aim to connect with at least ten individuals. Space out these conversations so you can reflect and refine your approach between each one.

5. Capture the Gold

Track everything. Create a matrix to map out what they shared, what inspired you, and what aligns with your values. Identify patterns and priorities.

6. Build a Strategy and Find a Mentor

Use what you've learned to craft your own #1R roadmap. If one of your interviewees stands out, ask them to mentor you. Be respectful, be prepared, and be coachable.

If they charge a fee—consider it an investment. Often, the right guidance can multiply your income, confidence, and clarity. What you gain will far outweigh the cost.

Repeat the Process, Evolve the Journey

Some mentors will be long-term. Others might help you unlock a single level. Either way, remember this:

Some of our greatest ideas come from the thoughts of others.

Bill Allen

Stay curious. Be bold. Take ownership of your identity and reputation. Because no one ever became extraordinary by staying safe, silent, or the same.

Redefine your reputation. Rebuild your identity. Align it with your values—and make it unshakable.

Greatness is not a possibility—it's a responsibility.

Greatness Awaits.

CHAPTER 2

DEFINING A #1REPUTATION

#1

CHAPTER 2
DEFINING A #1REPUTATION

It starts with Trust

We Talk About Reputation All the Time—But Do We Really Understand It?

You've heard it before:

- "They've got the best reputation"

- "I wouldn't go near them—their reputation's terrible"

- "I think I've heard their reputation is ... okay?"

It's casual, everyday language. We talk about reputation constantly—whether we're hiring a service provider, making a purchase, or choosing who to work with. It's always present in our thoughts when making a significant purchase, are they the right company.

But when you pause to really consider it, **what actually defines a #1R?**

I've asked this question in boardrooms, conference rooms, off-site retreats and one-on-one coaching sessions. I've asked top-tier companies with extraordinary reputations—and those struggling to rebuild theirs. And while responses vary, one word always surfaces.

Trust.

Trust is the foundation. It's the thread that runs through every great reputation. It's more than a feeling—it's the reliable result of one powerful behaviour:

Trust is doing what you say you will do.

This distinction is critical. Without trust, there can be no enduring reputation. With it, you create the conditions for influence, loyalty, and long-term success.

The Data Behind a 10/10 Reputation

We've interviewed hundreds of thousands of customers—real time customer interviews—defining the exceptional traits behind a **10/10 experience**, and one truth is clear:

Brilliant reputations are built on behaviour, not branding

A reputation of excellence lives in the way your people show up. We've identified two core categories that shape reputation:

1. Head Drivers (Logic-Based)

- Knowledge
- Systems
- Process accuracy

- Availability of stock

- Ease of purchase

- Clear documentation

- Convenient access

These are logical, left-brain factors. They're essential—but not enough.

2. Heart Drivers (Emotion-Based)

- Care and empathy

- Friendly, human communication

- Knowing the customer by name

- Personalisation

- Trustworthiness

- Going above and beyond

- Understanding their business

These are what make a business **memorable**. They make people feel seen, understood, and valued: they're what your customers will talk about long after the transaction is complete.

You can't fake a 10/10 experience. You can't "perform" trust. Being "nice" isn't enough. It must be **authentic**, driven by a culture of integrity and human connection.

Service Mindset Starts with the Team

How does your team *really* think about customer service?

Are they trained to execute tasks—or inspired to deliver moments of impact?

A #1R business prioritises **powerful communication** and helps its team understand not just what the customer needs, but **who the customer is**. It's about building trust, showing genuine friendliness, and being proactively helpful.

Even on an average day, encountering one person who delivers an exceptional experience can change everything. You've likely felt this—someone treats you like you're their only customer, goes out of their way to help, and makes your life easier. It's transformative. It's unforgettable.

When those behaviours are defined, taught, and reinforced across your business, you unlock a system for consistent excellence.

Of course, helpfulness looks different in different contexts. A five-minute transaction in a supply warehouse isn't the same as an architect designing someone's dream home. But in both, the **intention and behaviour behind the interaction** is what defines the experience.

Strategy Meets Emotion: Building from Your Reputation Edge

Some companies already have reputations for innovation, efficiency, or product quality. That's their edge. The smartest companies **build strategically** on that edge. They don't take it for granted—they lean into it, shape it, and scale it.

Every business must identify and nurture its edge. To do that, reputation must be part of your **strategic plan**—tied to leadership behavior, company culture, and customer expectations.

So ask yourself:

- What does your market require from your team in terms of service excellence?

- What behaviors make your company exceptional?

- What does it *look* and *feel* like to be the #1 supplier your customer works with?

Even if your customer deals with 50 other vendors, your goal is to become the **#1 they think of, trust, and prefer**.

You don't get there by guessing. You need real **CX research**. You need to know the truth.

"I Wish Others Were Like You"

When I work with teams, I often ask:

"Have you ever had a customer say,

'I wish others were like you'?"

Great companies can always say yes. But surprisingly, most can't clearly articulate what the customer actually meant. It's critical that you can articulate this to your team.

This is a missed opportunity.

That phrase is the ultimate compliment. It means the customer is **benchmarking you against everyone else**—and you've come out on top.

Next time you hear it, lean in. Ask:

"That's amazing to hear—can you share what stood out for you?"

Document their answer. Share it with your team. Turn it into a case study. Use it to define what your 10/10 reputation looks like in action.

Only your **customers** can tell you what a #1R is. Your job is to listen—and then design your strategy with their feedback at the core.

Don't Confuse Satisfaction with Loyalty

Many companies stop at customer satisfaction. They think, "We're doing fine. People seem happy." But satisfaction is not the goal. It's just a few steps above average—and it creates a dangerous **false sense of security**. You must have a library of 10/10 service stories to share, your team must understand how greatness looks and feels.

Our research focuses on something deeper: **Customer Appreciation**.

Appreciation creates emotional connection. It includes:

- Helpfulness

- Friendliness

- Trust

- Support

- Empathy

- Deep understanding

- Outstanding communication

When your customers **appreciate** you, they don't just return. They **recommend**. They defend your brand. They work with you, not just buy from you.

Appreciation is the heart of loyalty. It's what moves people from passive satisfaction to **active advocacy**.

#1R Starts Inside the Business

To build a #1 Reputation in the market, it must first exist **within** the business.

Your team must become the #1R **for each other**—collaborating, resolving issues, taking responsibility, and refusing to settle for average. They must seek proactive solutions, not just react to problems.

Culture is the cradle for reputation

When working together is structured, intentional, and values-driven—it becomes automatic to carry that same energy into the marketplace.

You can't fake this. You can't script it.

A true 10/10 experience is rooted in who your team is *being*, not just what they *do*. It's earned, not engineered. And it's built with the **highest level of integrity**.

So ask yourself:

- Are your team members clear on what a 10/10 experience looks like?

- Do they have the mindset to deliver appreciation, not just satisfaction?

- Are they empowered to take ownership of their behaviors, actions, and reputation?

Because in the end, a #1 Reputation is not a label. It's a legacy. One that's built moment by moment, interaction by interaction, and decision by decision.

Closing Thought:

Define It, Build It, Live It

You don't need to wonder what your reputation is.

You just need to **listen to your market**, define the behaviours that create impact, and build the systems to reinforce them.

A #1R is **earned** through consistency.

It's **designed** with intention.

And it's **lived** by the people who believe in the covenant (see chapter 3)

Reputation isn't a brand asset. It's your *identity in the world*. And when built with trust, value, and authenticity—it becomes your most powerful force in business and in life.

Greatness Awaits

CHAPTER 3
THE COVENANT

CHAPTER 3
THE COVENANT

Beyond the Wall – The Power of the Reputation Covenant Wallpaper or Culture?

Walk into almost any company reception, and you'll see them—those bold declarations of identity.

Framed and polished. Vision. Mission. Values. Crafted by consultants, approved by executives, and placed in pride of position on the wall.

They look great. They sound even better.

They are carefully worded to inspire, aspirational, poetic, positive.

But here's the uncomfortable question every leader must ask: **Are they lived… or just laminated?**

Because in most businesses, those statements are little more than wallpaper. They decorate the reception but fail to direct the culture. They inspire on the wall but disappear in the halls.

And here's the bitter truth: if you study the companies that collapsed under the weight of scandal, failure, or dysfunction, you'll still find those framed declarations in their reception. The words were there. But the integrity behind them was not.

That's the difference between wallpaper and culture.

The Gap Leaders Don't Want to See

When I first meet a leadership team, I'll often ask: *"Tell me about your vision and mission. How were they created? How do they show up in your customer experience, in your reputation, in your culture?"*

Too often, I get blank looks. Or generic answers. Or the dreaded, "I haven't been here long enough."

Think about that. If these words are truly the foundation of the business, why aren't they etched into every induction, every team meeting, every decision? Why aren't they so alive that even the newest recruit can explain them with pride?

I've even sat with executives whose sole job is people and culture and they've struggled to connect the slogans with actual behaviour.

That's the danger. And it's consistent across industries:

There's a disconnect between what's on the wall and what's lived in the hall.

Reputation starts with Clarity

Your reputation is your most valuable asset. It never takes a day off. It's entirely built, carried, and protected by your people.

Which means your culture cannot be symbolic. It has to be structural. It has to be more than words.

To achieve a #1Reputation (#1R), you need something that lives in the DNA of the company. Something more binding than a slogan. More actionable than a value statement. More enduring than a glossy poster.

You need a **Covenant.**

The Covenant: A New Cultural Distinction

After decades of research, reflection, and customer insights, one thing became clear: The next evolution beyond vision, mission, and values is something deeper. Something human. Something that protects Reputation.

I call it **The Reputation Covenant.**

"A promise sanctioned by an oath."

Your Covenant is not branding. It's not a campaign. It's a living promise to every person your business touches— inside and outside.

It reflects your culture, your integrity, your values. But more importantly, it creates accountability. It's not written to inspire shareholders or decorate receptions. It's written for meaning, for action, for alignment.

And when a team co-creates it, something powerful happens. The atmosphere shifts. The language changes. People stop talking about the company as "they" and start talking as "we."

A Covenant is not about performance. It's about identity. It's your team saying:

"This is who we are. This is what we stand for. This is the promise we make, and the oath we live by."

Why the Covenant Works

The brilliance of a Covenant lies in its ability to cut through complexity. It's not another statement dreamed up by marketing consultants. It's not a tick-box compliance exercise.

It's lived, because it's created together.

The process itself is as valuable as the outcome:

- It requires honesty, trust, and vulnerability

- It forces conversations that rarely happen

- It surfaces contradictions between what's preached and what's practiced

- It aligns people in a way a slogan never can

And once it exists, it becomes a compass. Not for good times, but for hard ones. When pressure is high, when values are tested, when customers are demanding, when markets are shifting—the Covenant holds true.

It isn't fragile like a mission statement. It's durable like an oath.

The Structure: Promise + Oath

A Covenant is built on two sentences. Simple, but profound:

1   **The Promise** (what we will do): Begins with *"To…"*

2   **The Oath** (who we will be): Begins with *"We…"*

The Promise defines your commitment.
The Oath defines your character.

Together, they form a declaration of identity—authored by the team, for the team, and lived every day.

A Real-World Example

During the chaos of the COVID-era building crisis, I worked with a home-building company under immense pressure. The industry was drowning in complaints: communication failures, unmet expectations, company collapses everywhere.

Instead of falling into the same trap, this company chose to create their Covenant.

They brought their people together. Flip charts. Post-its. Hours of raw, honest dialogue. Who are we? What do we stand for? What do we promise? How do we want to be seen?

They didn't rush. They worked on it for weeks.

And the final Covenant was simple, powerful, unforgettable:

"At [Company], our promise is clear: To be accommodating, communicate effectively, and deliver an exceptional experience. We are your supportive, professional team, working together seamlessly to bring your vision to life."

The effect?

- Record sales and margins

- Explosive referral growth

- Suppliers prioritising them as #1

- Staff retention soaring

- A pipeline that screamed market leadership

The owner's reflection was telling:

"My job now is to get out of the way—support the team, provide the resources, and let them do what they've committed to."

That's the power of a Covenant-led culture.

What a Covenant Creates

When done right, a Covenant doesn't just live on paper. It lives in people. It:

- Inspires questions

- Sparks conversations

- Tells a story

- Builds pride

- Aligns identity

- Creates unity

It becomes the invisible glue holding the company together—and the visible difference customers feel in every interaction.

Imagine This

Pause and imagine:

- Your team aligned behind a Covenant they created, not one handed to them

- Your culture so clear that even the newest recruit can articulate it with pride

- Customers saying, "We trust them, because they live what they say"

- Suppliers prioritising you, because they know who you are and what you stand for

- A prospect asking about your Covenant—and you telling the story of how it was born

That one conversation could win you business that competitors can't even access.

Closing Reflection

Vision and mission still have a role. But they're no longer enough.

The Covenant goes further:

- It's not about words on a wall. It's about culture in motion

- It's not written for marketing. It's written for meaning

- It's not executive-led. It's team-owned

- It's not something you preach. It's something you practice

Your Covenant is not a message. It's a movement.
It unites your team. It inspires your market. It builds a reputation competitors cannot compete with.

So, the real question is:

Are you ready to create your Covenant? Are you ready to build something that lives long beyond slogans—and shapes your legacy as a #1R company?

Because the companies that do will not only win trust. They'll define it.

Greatness Awaits.

CHAPTER 4

THE POWER OF YES

#1

CHAPTER 4
THE POWER OF YES

Building a Reputation That Can't Be Ignored

A Culture That Says "Yes"

A #**1R** is not built by being known for saying *No*.
"No" is easy.
"Yes" takes work.

Saying no is easy. It's safe. It lets you stick to the manual, avoid hard work, and move on. But **a reputation is not built in moments of convenience**—it's built in moments of pressure. And the pressure point is where the **possibility of "Yes"** lives and a world class reputation is forged.

You can quickly assess a company's cultural standards just by looking at its customer feedback—specifically, how the business responds to non-standard or high-effort customer requests. High-value customers, in particular, don't ask for something unless it matters. If they're asking, it's important to them. That moment is a test—not just of service—but of **intent**.

And too often it's a missed opportunity.

When "No" Is a Reflex, Reputation Suffers

How many times have you heard these phrases?

- "Sorry, we don't do that"

- "No, that's not part of our product range"

- "Unfortunately, that's outside our scope"

These may be valid answers—but they often reflect a **lazy mindset**, not a thoughtful solution. Especially when spoken to a loyal or high-value customer.

A request outside your standard protocol is **not** an inconvenience— it's an opportunity.

If your cultural standard is built around *finding a way to Yes*, your team is conditioned to pause, assess, collaborate, and think creatively. This is where innovation is born. This is where relationships are strengthened. This is where **loyalty is earned**.

Innovation Begins With a Question

Creating a culture of "Yes" doesn't mean saying yes to everything. It means starting from a place of **possibility**, not resistance. It means asking:

- How might we help?

- Who else could assist?

- What's one small step toward a solution?

Even when a direct Yes isn't possible, the intent behind the response matters. Consider this difference:

"Sorry, we don't offer that."

Versus

"That's not something we typically offer, but leave it with me—I'll see what I can do."

The second response builds **trust**. It shows care. It makes your customer feel **seen**. Even if the ultimate outcome is still a "no," the **experience** is one of effort, partnership, and service.

One is a wall. The other is a door.

The Ripple Effect of a "Yes" Mindset

Here's what happens when your team makes the effort to find a way to Yes:

- You solve your customer's challenge

- You potentially create a new partnership or revenue stream

- You deepen the trust in your relationship

- You set yourself apart from the competition

- You show that your reputation isn't a slogan - it's an identity

Even better? When you refer a customer to someone else who *can* help, you're still serving with excellence. You've created value. You've helped someone, and in doing so you've likely opened the door to **reciprocity**.

Saying Yes builds momentum.

Saying No shuts it down.

What Happens Internally When You Default to "No"

This isn't just about external customer service. Saying No becomes a **reflex inside the company**, too.

One of the most common issues post-COVID has been a decline in productivity—not due to a lack of effort, but because of a cultural shift toward "busy = overwhelmed." In that state, saying No becomes an automatic defence mechanism.

But that mindset creates barriers between departments. It fuels silos. It breaks down collaboration. It limits growth. You can measure this in your business.

Ask yourself:

- How often do managers default to "No"?

- How many departments have rigid processes that can't flex?

- How many times is No said without exploring an alternative?

- Are your most curious, creative people being heard—or drowned out by gatekeepers?

In our audits, leaders are often shocked by how many key people say No as a first response—because it's easier, faster, or more justifiable.

But easy doesn't build a #1R.

Say Yes to Opportunity, Not to Chaos

Let's be clear: Not every request deserves a Yes. There are times when No is the right and responsible answer.

But in ten typical No scenarios, how many could be re-evaluated? How many could lead to innovation, process improvement, or unexpected partnership?

Even getting halfway to Yes is still progress.

- It shows customers you're trying

- It shows your team you care

- It shows the market that you're agile and responsive

That effort alone builds loyalty.

"Yes" Builds Character. "No" Builds Distance.

Your greatest breakthroughs didn't come from easy situations. They came from friction—when someone said, "We don't know how, but let's figure it out."

"Yes" makes you stronger.
It makes you **resilient**.
It forces learning, collaboration, and growth.

"No," used as a shield, can make you lazy.
It builds walls, not bridges.
It's forgettable at best—and damaging at worst.

Want a powerful way to build a #1R?

Make Yes your default mindset.

The Elon Musk Principle

Elon Musk is one of the most visible modern examples of a "Yes" thinker.

SpaceX. Tesla. Neuralink. The Boring Company. xAI.

All of these companies began as ideas the world said "No" to. Impossible. Impractical. Unachievable.

Yet Musk—and his teams—found a way to Yes. They pushed boundaries. They broke moulds. They asked better questions. And they created solutions that redefined entire industries.

You don't have to launch rockets to adopt the mindset. You simply need to **refuse to settle for the easy way out**.

Take the "Yes" Challenge

Here's how to get started:

1. Audit Your Culture

- Where in your business are you hearing "No" too often? Which department and what's their reason?

- What are the most common types of customer requests that get denied? This is critical to know: it's directly linked to revenue and retention. What if you're driving customers away without even knowing it?

- Are you defaulting to No—or defaulting to problem-solving? It's very risky to allow your team to determine what's possible from their opinion or attitude

2. Identify Your Gatekeepers

- Who controls decision-making? Are they a glass half full or half empty?

- Are they collaborative, curious, solution-oriented?

- Or do they protect the status quo? Or protect themselves by resisting change?

3. Recognise the Seekers

- Who in your team keeps asking questions? Observe the responses they receive. Are they being shut down?

- Who looks for options, alternatives, or ways to serve? Who are these innovators of service?

- Elevate them. Empower them. Make it known you seek those who think

4. Redefine "Yes" in Your Business

- Create a culture of *earned Yes*, not *automatic No*. Review decisions and have the team understand the thinking process to the conclusion of Yes/No

- Recognise and reward those who go the extra mile to find solutions. Celebrate the thinkers and those who take action

Closing Thoughts:

The Yes That Builds Your Future

Imagine if your customers described your business like this:

"They always try to help. Even when they can't say yes, they never shut us down, they always look for solutions and suggestions"

That's a business people come back to. That's a business people refer. That's a business that earns a #**1 Reputation**.

So ask yourself:

- How many "No's" could you turn into a "Yes"? How can you shift the mindset towards Yes?

- How many new opportunities are waiting just beyond the easy answer? What if there's another 10% revenue gain available now?

Say Yes to learning.
Say Yes to problem-solving.
Say Yes to serving.
Say Yes to building something worth remembering.

Greatness Awaits—it starts with a single word, say it often, say it with intention, say it by being of service. **Say Yes.**

CHAPTER 5

THE THREE PILLARS OF REPUTATION

#1

CHAPTER 5
THE THREE PILLARS OF REPUTATION

The Foundation of Market Leadership

Reputation Is a System Approach

There are three pillars of reputation, each critical to securing and maintaining the #1 position in any market. While these pillars are always in motion, many companies underestimate their combined impact on the synergy of a high-performing organisation.

Reputation is often misunderstood as the outcome of good branding or clever marketing. But in reality, reputation is a **strategic system**—a living, breathing force that drives culture, innovation, revenue, margin, loyalty, and competitive advantage.

In high-performing companies, reputation doesn't just happen. It's intentionally built and relentlessly protected through three distinct, interconnected areas: **Suppliers, Team, and Customers**. These are the **Three Pillars of Reputation**.

Each pillar plays a critical role in shaping how your business is perceived—and whether it earns the elusive status of being the **#1 Most Trusted** in its market. For many companies the interconnected relationships are misunderstood, they must work in synergy to ensure service excellence and a #1R

Let's explore each pillar, how it contributes to your reputation, and the steps required to master them.

Pillar 1: The Supply Chain – Your External Backbone

The Covid era revealed a brutal truth: a company is only as strong as the weakest link in its supply chain. Many companies failed to identify their risks in supply chain and Covid just confirmed the reality for many, it shouldn't take a shock to the system before its value is realised. When global supply was constrained, businesses with strong supplier relationships were prioritised. Others were left waiting, often at the cost of customer trust and significant revenue.

This was a wake-up call. And it illustrated a core truth of the reputation economy: **Your supply chain is not separate from your reputation—it's a direct reflection of it.** There were many who were dealt a severe hit and it was the result of long-term beliefs: they were the customer and the supplier should be grateful. However if your attitude was average, you paid invoices late, didn't see suppliers as critical and treated poorly then you got dumped down the priority list.

High-reputation companies—what we call **#1R companies**—don't leave supplier relationships to chance. They:

- Work proactively to become the **#1 customer** for each supplier. They plan to be important

- Recognise that effort, clarity, communication, respect, and support are what earn preferential treatment

- Treat their suppliers the same way they treat their most valued customers

Here's a mindset shift to consider: How much effort does your team put into retaining top customers? Now imagine if your suppliers felt just as valued. The result? Better service, stronger support, and a powerful competitive edge.

#1R companies go further. They **audit supplier performance** and **invite feedback in both directions**. They evaluate:

- Are our suppliers meeting agreed standards? Do you have standards and agreements?

- Do our suppliers clearly understand their role in protecting our reputation?

- How well are we, as a customer, making it easy for them to serve us?

In best-practice businesses, suppliers are embedded into the growth plan. They're informed when new customers come onboard, especially referrals, aligned with delivery expectations, and aware of what's at stake. Nothing is left to interpretation.

To complete the loop, #1R companies survey their suppliers to understand how they can be a 10/10 customer. Yes—they ask the people they pay how well *they're* doing. This sends a powerful message: "We make it easy for you to serve us, so we expect the same in return."

This is not about control—it's about **mutual respect and partnership**. When your suppliers are invested in your success, reputation becomes a shared responsibility. Don't you want your most valued customers partnering with you and sharing their growth plan? So why wouldn't you do it in reverse?

Pillar 2: The Team – Your Internal Reputation Champions

If the supply chain is your external backbone, your **team** is your internal engine—and the stewards of your daily reputation. Every member of your team is either protecting, building, maintaining, or damaging your reputation—whether they know it or not. That's the challenge: **most don't know.**

In keynotes and workshops, I often ask leaders, "If I spoke to every person in your business, would I hear consistent, aligned answers about how they protect the company's reputation?"

Very few answer "yes". Most leave it to assumption and the vision and mission statements!

Reputation responsibility isn't just for executives. It belongs to **everyone**—from front-line staff to leadership. Every role connects to customer experience in some way, the internal and external customer.

Consider the example of a warehouse manager I worked with. Initially, he saw his role as disconnected from sales or customer relationships. But when we walked through the journey of a delivery truck arriving and how critical his responsibilities were— You're on schedule for them, clear access, accurate paperwork, helpful staff, safe loading, clean facilities—it became clear that **he** was the first point of contact for many external partners. His team shaped their perception of the professionalism and reliability of the company. How does he make his warehouse the #1 for all transport companies? It now became personal, and his professional reputation was equally on the line. He changed his mindset and reinvented his role. He took the challenge to have the #1 warehouse for pick-up and delivery drivers.

That realisation changed everything. When your team understands their individual contributions to the customer experience and the company's broader goals, they rise to the occasion.

At a construction company I coach, even the labourers embraced their role as "directors of first impressions." They kept job sites spotless and secure, held all the trades and suppliers accountable for cleanliness because they knew it spoke volumes to reputation. The result? customers were impressed at the standards of cleanliness and order, competitors were left behind, and the labouring team became a respected part of the company. They see themselves as a part of the sales force. Why? Because their professionalism caused a sale, a new customer noted they were watching all the builders in the estate and their site was always impeccable.

When people understand how their work contributes to the company's reputation—and why that matters—they rise to meet the standard. **They shift from doing a job to owning a responsibility.**

Every team member should be able to answer two questions with clarity:

1. How do I contribute to the company's reputation?

2. What does a 10/10 experience look like in my role?

If your team can't answer these, it's not their fault—it's a **leadership gap**. Your job is to close it.

Pillar 3: The Customer – The Final Judge of Reputation

Ultimately, your reputation is not what you say it is—it's what your customers **believe** it is.

Too many businesses rely on internal assumptions or outdated feedback methods to gauge customer experience. The reality is, in B2B especially, most new customers come **only when a competitor fails**. You're often not the first choice—you're the replacement.

The lag between opportunity and revenue can be months, even years. During that time, your team, processes, and suppliers must deliver flawlessly. Otherwise, the cost of acquisition becomes a loss.

Reputation is the **X-factor in market valuation**, customer loyalty, and long-term growth, but achieving "#1 reputation" status isn't about occasional good service. It requires **rigorous, structured research** that gets to the heart of what your market values.

Generic online surveys won't cut it. Experience and expertise in how to obtain high qualitative feedback and analysis is critical You need:

- Tailored interview questions that uncover what customers **really** think and want

- Deep insights across all dimensions: experience, trust, service delivery, value, communication, referrals, and comparison to competitors are a part of the strategy

- A framework that links data to action, with key responsibilities and KPI's

Your reputation lives in your customers' minds. If you don't know what's in there, you can't manage or influence it. You can't let your competitors get into their minds.

Who Owns Reputation?

Reputation is your company's most valuable asset—but only when it's **actively managed**.

In elite organisations, the three pillars of reputation are not abstract ideas. They are owned, measured, and led by specific people.

So let's make it real:

- **Who owns your supplier reputation?**

- **Who is responsible for your team reputation?**

- **Who manages your market reputation?**

If your answer is "the CEO," you've got a problem. The CEO can lead and report—but ownership must be distributed across the business.

Your Challenge:

Rate each of your three pillars—Supplier, Team, and Customer—on a scale of 1 to 10.
Where are you strongest? Where are you vulnerable? And most importantly, **who is accountable for improving them?**

Reputation doesn't manage itself. But when it's built across all three pillars—with clarity, structure, and leadership—it becomes your greatest strategic advantage.

CHAPTER 6

THE FOUR LEVELS OF REPUTATION

#1

CHAPTER 6
THE FOUR LEVELS OF REPUTATION

From Risk to Reverence

Reputation Is Strategy

Reputation is not a marketing concept. It's not a "nice-to-have" by-product of good branding or clever campaigns. Reputation is strategy (or it should be), and in today's hyper-competitive business world it's the most critical currency you own. The reality is your current state of reputation is the result of past strategy; can you track the journey?

But here's the problem: most organisations treat reputation like something that simply happens to them, instead of something they intentionally build. They fail to recognise that reputation has levels—and where you are on that scale determines how your team behaves, how your suppliers respond, and how your customers buy (or don't).

The are four levels of reputation—risk, build & protect, 10/10 excellence, and #1 most trusted—and how they apply across your three essential pillars, Team, Suppliers, and Customers, determines the current state of your business relationships.

It's vital you understand where your business sits on the reputation ladder—and more importantly, how to climb it.

Level 1: Risk – The Silent Reputation Killer

Risk is the most underestimated element of reputation. It often goes unnoticed until it's too late—until a key customer walks away, a team member quits unexpectedly, or your supply chain collapses without warning. By then, you're in damage control mode.

As the old saying goes:

"It takes 10 years to build a reputation and one moment to destroy it."

Reputation risk shows up in subtle but deadly ways:

- A new team member telling a major customer "no" without understanding their business needs and your high level relationship. Does this happen in your team?

- Miscommunication with a supplier causing delivery delays. Immediate impact on your reputation and how you are perceived.

- A leader failing to grasp team history, leading to disengagement and breakdowns. How do you ensure your culture is safe?

Wherever there is risk, there is reputational damage. And often, you don't see the effects until the consequences are already in motion. At this level, your primary goal is to identify and contain the risks—before they cost you more than you can afford.

Level 2: Build and Protect – The Foundation of Stability

Once you've addressed immediate risks, your focus now shifts to building and protecting your reputation. This is the foundation of consistency—where satisfaction is predictable and relationships become more secure. At this stage, your reputation score is typically around 8/10 satisfaction. That's good—but not good enough to relax. You're no longer in crisis mode, but you must stay alert. How do you ensure the team is always in protection mode? Do they know what to look/listen for?

This is where reputation repair begins.

Key principles at this level:

- **Clarity leads to power**: Customise your communication and support. A one-size-fits-all approach won't work here. What is the communication protocol for your team? Since it varies between each pillar, is it a defined process and standard, and is it measured against 10/10?

- Follow-up and Accountability: Every interaction should be intentional, tracked, and reviewed. It must have a commitment to serve, and everyone is responsible for their performance and outcome

- Team Education: Train your team on what excellence looks like—don't assume they already know. Most people are trained to believe that satisfaction is the goal, a #1R company has satisfaction at the minimum starting point. What's the belief in your team? It's poor leadership to assume the team all have clarity of what excellence looks like

Anything below 8/10 is considered reputation risk. Your goal is to get every stakeholder—internal and external—into the "build and protect" zone and ready for the next level.

Level 3: 10/10 Excellence – Reputation as a Key Performance Driver

At the 10/10 level, reputation becomes a competitive advantage. This is where your business begins to differentiate itself—not just in service or product, but in behaviour and culture. You have a new identity that aligns with the beliefs and expectations of high quality.

Let's explore what 10/10 excellence looks like across your three pillars:

Suppliers

- Proactively introduce new opportunities to you. They have a vested interest in your success and actively seek efficiency improvements for you

- Give you priority access to products and innovations. They want you to be cutting edge where possible and offer you the latest innovations to help you grow

- Consider you a valued partner and advocate for your business in their networks. Your success is immediately theirs, and of course you will deal with them when they refer

Team

- Align deeply with company goals and values. Enhance the culture by being the example for others to follow

- Operate with initiative, loyalty, and a winning mindset, always looking for the 1% improvements; living and breathing your Covenant

- Act as brand ambassadors—proud to refer, represent, and protect the company

- Team turnover is low and high performance is the standard. There is a true common goal

Customers

- Feel a strong connection to your team and brand. They have personal connection with the team and genuinely care for each other

- Are open about their needs and trust you to deliver. They will share their business plans and objectives

- Accept your terms, respect your value, and offer full wallet share

- Actively refer you—even risking their own reputation in the process. They trust you will protect their name and do your best to serve

At 10/10, the difference is emotional. Loyalty is no longer transactional—it's relational. People don't just buy from you— they believe in you. It's a connection that's beyond marketing: it's personal.

Level 4: #1 Most Trusted – The Reputation Summit

Reaching the level of #1 Most Trusted is rare. At this level, you become the benchmark. You are the company others are measured against. Your reputation is no longer just part of your brand—it is your brand. When your company is mentioned, it's immediately associated with being the best.

Here's how this level shows up across your ecosystem:

Supply Chain

- Suppliers never let you down—no matter what. You never have the need to be concerned. The boss personally has an eye on your care

- You're their reference client, their priority, and their pride. They use your name as bragging rights

- In times of shortage, they go to extraordinary lengths to protect your business—even buying from competitors to keep you supplied

Team

- Team members wear your logo like a badge of honour. They are true ambassadors of the company

- Your company is considered the best place to work in your industry

- Training, tools, culture, and compensation are world-class. You are the standard

- You have a waiting list of talent. Key hires seek you out. You are a magnet for the champions

Customers

- Loyalty is unshakable. They rely on you for success in their own business

- They give you honest feedback, support your innovations, and actively champion your brand. You will a part of their sales process around quality

- They understand that your value isn't cheap—but it pays

- Your customer base becomes your most powerful marketing asset

This level is not accidental. It's the result of diligent reputation engineering across every touchpoint. And the benefits are extraordinary: market power, pricing strength, brand equity, future-proof growth and the highest company valuation.

Auditing Your Reputation: Measuring What Matters

So, how do you know where your business sits on the reputation ladder? Simple: measure it. Relying on opinions is dangerous. You need a structured scorecard across all three pillars: Team, Suppliers, and Customers. There are various forms of experience measurements available, most are web based and can be helpful, however for high value relationships across all three pillars you need accurate feedback and metrics. Experience is key to any success, ensuring you have the correct process and experience operating it is essential.

Visit www.1reputation.net to download ready-made audits. These are designed to assist you in creating measurements and benchmarking.

These audits help you identify:

- Where you're at risk

- Where you're in the "build and protect" zone

- Where you've reached 10/10 excellence

- Where you're the market leader in trust

Assign ownership of each audit pillar. This shouldn't fall solely on the CEO: they need the results to act upon. Use it as a leadership development tool—empower rising stars to lead the process and report on progress.

Supplier Audit – Are You a Priority or an Afterthought?

Ask yourself:

- Are we a valued partner—or a transactional client?

- Do suppliers bring us ideas—or do we chase them down?

- Are we holding on to legacy relationships that no longer serve us?

Key benchmarks:

- Risk: Poor communication, outdated technology, inconsistent service

- Build & Protect: Decent terms and reliability, but not top priority

- 10/10: You're well-known internally, and the relationship is strong

- #1 Most Trusted: Supply is guaranteed—even in crisis. You're irreplaceable

Team Audit – The Pulse of Internal Reputation

Your internal reputation determines how your people show up every day.

Key benchmarks:

- Risk (7/10 and below): High turnover, low morale, disengagement, low productivity

- Build & Protect: New policies and process help restore trust. Team begins to align

- 10/10: Culture is strong. People thrive and contribute meaningfully and innovate process

- #1 Most Trusted: Talent lines up to join. The market raves about your team. Your culture is the most powerful weapon your competitors can't match

Use these insights to strengthen leadership, improve systems, and align the team with the company's mission.

Customer Audit – The Voice of the Market

Your market reputation is your business's valuation multiplier. It determines not just your revenue—but your future revenue. It's the window into the DNA of your company; all roads lead here.

Key benchmarks:

- Risk: Low loyalty, price sensitivity, no referral pipeline, customer acquisition is expensive, customers are challenging to deal with

- Build & Protect: Solid base, but still competing heavily for wallet share, not standing out in the market

- 10/10: You are the preferred supplier. Value is measured by trust, not cost, your reputation is strong and respected

- #1 Most Trusted: You're a strategic partner, not just a vendor. You shape their growth, customer acquisition is lowest possible cost, conversion rates optimal

Use customer insights to innovate, build predictable KPI's, prioritise opportunity, and build a market that works for you.

Reputation Is Everyone's Responsibility

Reputation doesn't live in the marketing department. It's not owned by the sales team or the CEO. It lives in every interaction, every system, and every person in your business.

Your journey from risk to #1 most trusted will not happen overnight. But it will happen—if you make reputation a strategic priority. Every #1 company has worked a strategic plan to get there, and the team are clear on the responsibilities they have in achieving the goals.

So, ask yourself:

- Where do we stand across each pillar and how do we score?

- Who owns each area of reputation, who holds the primary responsibility?

- What actions are we taking to measure and improve, who's responsible?

The companies who thrive in the future will be those who treat reputation not as a byproduct—but as a strategic asset. The most powerful and valuable commodity the company holds.

CHAPTER 7

STRATEGIC FOUNDATIONS FOR A #1REPUTATION

CHAPTER 7

STRATEGIC FOUNDATIONS FOR A #1REPUTATION

Building the Employer of Choice

To earn a **#1 Reputation (#1R)** and be recognised as the employer of choice, a company must have a **clearly defined, well-executed strategy**. While that might sound complex, the core principles are straightforward when broken down.

From the **internal team perspective**, there are three fundamental pillars:

1. **Recruitment and onboarding**

2. **Ongoing training and development**

3. **Measuring and rewarding high performance**

Your people control your most valuable asset—your reputation. So, the question becomes:

How do you ensure every team member is in the right mindset to protect and elevate it?

This is where many businesses go wrong. Too often, **HR professionals are consumed by compliance and operational issues**, leaving little time to focus on cultural leadership or reputation-building. This is why the role of a **Chief Reputation Officer (CRO)** becomes so valuable (see Chapter 17).

In a #1R company, **being a great colleague matters just as much as doing a great job**. You're not just building a team of champions—you're building a **championship team**.

Recruitment Is Just the Beginning

Recruitment today presents unique challenges. Even finding candidates with baseline suitability can be difficult. But the real measure of success begins with **onboarding**.

I often ask leaders:

What does your onboarding process look like at 1 week, 2 weeks, 30 days, and 60 days?

Not just tasks and technical skills—but:

- Who is this person being?
- Are they showing character?
- Are they taking responsibility?
- Are they following through on commitments?
- Are they maintaining a professional mindset?

Skills can be taught. But **mindsets must be assessed**—and too few companies have a structured approach to evaluating that during onboarding.

Embedding Culture into Strategy

Your strategic plan must include **ongoing cultural training**.

As outlined in the chapter on **Generalised Principles**, world-class teams are built on:

- Responsibility

- Integrity

- Character

- Accountability

- Proactive communication

- Beliefs

These aren't just traits—they're **non-negotiable standards**.

Cultural excellence is not a function of HR alone. It must be embedded in the **leadership team's mindset and management style**. You must regularly assess not just what leaders are doing—but **who they are being**.

"No team can rise above the constraints of its leader."

If you wouldn't rehire a current leader today, that's a red flag. If the team senses that a leader lacks capability, high performers will leave—and the average will stay. That's not a high-performing culture. That's a slow slide toward mediocrity. That's where satisfaction lives.

Every leader must be crystal clear on their responsibility to build and protect the **internal customer's** reputation—the team.

Designing the #1R Customer Experience

Just as you need a plan for your team, you must have a strategic plan for your **external customers**.

It starts with one question:

What does a 10/10 experience look like for your business? You cannot ask within the team, you must ask the market, you must engage your customer.

Once you define it, you must **reverse engineer** the systems, training, communication, and journey mapping required to achieve it.

This is your most important strategic step.

Without it, you're guessing. Or worse—you're copying your competitors. And that rarely works.

Legendary business thinker W. Edwards Deming said:

> *"94% of business problems are process and system related. Only 6% are people-related."*

If you're not getting the results you want, look at your systems:

- Is the hiring process attracting the right talent?
- Does onboarding reinforce both skill and culture?
- Is training frequent and effective?

- Are managers mentoring and coaching, or just managing?

- Are you setting people up to win or leaving them to fail?

System gaps often show up as people problems. But the solution is strategic—not personal. It's easy to blame people, it's harder to improve the system.

Learn from the 10/10 — and the <8/10

Beyond designing the ideal experience, it's equally important to identify what's missing for customers who score you below 8/10.

Across thousands of customer interviews, our research shows two consistent gaps:

1. **Clear and consistent communication**

2. **Efficiency in delivery**

These are the top areas customers say need improvement—year after year.

Do you have a **communication protocol** within your business?

Do you have clear "rules of the game" for how your team communicates—internally and externally?

You must start internally. If your team isn't delivering a 10/10 experience for one another, they can't do it for customers. The good news? Internal communication is **easier to control, review, and improve**. And once it's working, it becomes the perfect blueprint for external communication.

A Communication Protocol That Builds Loyalty

Here's a simple, powerful rule:

A customer never contacts you twice for the same reason.

Once they've contacted you, it's your responsibility to take over. Be proactive. Keep them updated. Resolve the issue. Make it frictionless.

Imagine you deal with a company where you never have to chase them. You speak once—and after that, they take the lead.

Would you ever go anywhere else?

This standard is **rare in practice**—but when it's implemented, it becomes one of the greatest differentiators in business.

Design Touchpoints That Serve

Map out the ideal behaviours at **every customer touchpoint**. Recognise that some moments require more communication than others. Invite your customers into this process.

Ask them:

- "What does excellence look like to you?"

- "How can we be the best supplier or partner for you?"

They will tell you. And when you act on it, your reputation grows.

This simple act shows that you care, and more importantly, that you're committed to **being better for them**.

Efficiency in delivery

Your delivery process, product or service, will have multiple steps. From the start to the final step of customer experience. Are yours mapped out clearly for all to understand? Visual diagrams are the best for your team to understand and follow. Our research proves the breakdown is in the customer journey process and a particular step/s that cause lag, frustration, error, to mention a few. You can have the best communication but if you don't deliver as expected you still damage your reputation. There are really no excuses for efficiency issues, other than unique moments that we accept can occur. We never want a reputation for not keeping or word on efficiency. Consider the reputations of companies like Amazon who can move products around the world faster than the post office. The knowledge and technology is available for any business to learn how to improve.

The Role of the Chief Reputation Officer

The CRO (see chapter 12) ensures the entire business understands what matters—internally and externally. They help define the focus for each team and department and align everything around **building and protecting reputation**.

This isn't a vanity role. It's a strategic one.

Planning for Growth — Anywhere

Whether you're expanding into a new city, state, or country, you must have a **#1R strategy**.

Ask your leadership team:

- If we had to start again, what systems, culture, and communication protocols would we need?

- What kind of team would we hire?

- What mindset and leadership style would we demand?

- How would we measure success in the first 30, 60, and 90 days?

Have each leader build a department-level plan as if they were launching from scratch. Then—compare it to what you have now. What's missing? That gap is your **reputation roadmap**.

Closing Thoughts:

Build from the Future, Then Reverse Engineer

Strategic thinking doesn't always require reinvention. Sometimes, it's as simple as imagining what **great** looks like in a new environment—and working backward from there.

A #1 Reputation isn't built by default.

It's built by **design**.

CHAPTER 8

THE GENERALISED PRINCIPLES OF GREATNESS

#1

CHAPTER 8
THE GENERALISED PRINCIPLES OF GREATNESS

The foundation of a #1R culture

We never wake up needing proof that gravity exists or that the sun will rise in the morning. Some principles are simply **ever-present**, operating without question. The same is true in business dynamics. Principles—whether acknowledged or not—are always at play in your team, your leadership, your culture, and your reputation.

Over the last 20 years, as a coach and founder of **Saguity** my work with businesses ranging from billion-dollar enterprises to local veterinary clinics, I've relentlessly tested these **Generalised Principles** across businesses—some with hundreds of locations (company, franchise, dealership models), and others with just one. There are over 50 principles I can apply to a company, these are the top 4, they are the bedrock below the foundation.

It doesn't matter the size.
It doesn't matter the industry.
It doesn't matter the history.

These principles apply. Always.

In every company I work with, these principles are embedded into the team—whether delivered through workshops, keynotes, conferences, coaching, or mentoring—customised for every level of hierarchy.
The key variable?
Mindset.

Some people embrace these principles instantly and ignite their careers.
Others resist, defend their current reality, and block growth.
Over time, I learned:
You cannot predict who will rise.
It's not age, education, or even experience—it's personal mindset.
It's the internal story they choose to live by:

"Victim of circumstance"
or
"Architect of opportunity."

What matters most to you, as a leader, is this:
Regardless of how individuals respond, the collective engagement of your culture defines your reputation.
And your reputation—your #1R—is your greatest strategic asset.

Some of these principles you may have seen in my previous books—**The Client Revolution** and **The 10 Commandments of Client Appreciation**—but let's be clear:
This is a new context.

If you think of context as the **fruit bowl**, and content as the **fruit**, then this book presents a new bowl entirely—a new way to view what you hold, what you build, and what you protect.

Over the last 12 months, I've retested and refined these principles with both large corporate teams and small entrepreneurial ones.
The results have been **beyond expectation—**
creating new levels of team engagement, resilience, and reputation strength.

This chapter invites you—and your leadership team—to step back, reflect deeply, and ask:

- Where were we?

- Where are we?

- Where are we going?

- And who are we becoming along the way?

Because as a leader, you get to choose.
You shape your legacy.
Your culture and reputation are either **in motion—or in decline**.

You get to choose between: "I am" or "I was."

Studies show that **team engagement** is now the #1 challenge across industries.
And let's be blunt:
Post-2020, many companies are running on depleted resources—human and cultural.

The Great Resignation of 2021–22 ripped experience from organisations, leaving gaps that no resume could fill. Companies were forced to backfill with hope, best guesses, and urgent hires—often misaligned to the existing culture.

This seismic shift is a major contributor to the current lag in CX standards today.
And here's the hard truth:
Many leadership teams are simply surviving, not thriving.

The experience gap left in the building means new managers are spinning plates like circus performers:

- Desperately getting each one moving

- Trying to maintain momentum

- Hiding the crash when one falls

Mental fatigue is at an all-time high.
Leaders are exhausted trying to "cope"—let alone drive transformational CX improvements or think about achieving a #1 Reputation.

If this sounds familiar, it's likely not just an assumption that your reputation is at risk.
It's a reality in motion.
And if no one owns reputation management ...
If no one is actively measuring and protecting it ...
It will decline.
Guaranteed.

(We dive into this more deeply in the upcoming chapter: **The Chief Reputation Officer**.)

What Matters Most?

The ever-present, essential cultural distinctions.

The cultural heartbeat that must be alive and measurable if you are serious about building, protecting, and leveraging a #1Reputation.

Because reputation is not a marketing project.
It is not a slogan or a glossy poster in the lunchroom.
It's a living, breathing reflection of **your standards**, **your leadership**, and **your team's daily behaviours**.

The Generalised Principles of Greatness are not theories. They are natural laws in business—just like gravity. They are always operating, whether you see them or not.

The companies, teams, and leaders who thrive—the ones that become unshakable—are those who master these principles and lead from them every day.

Now, let's get into exactly what those principles are.

Because knowing the rules of gravity won't stop you from falling... but knowing the **principles of greatness** will stop your business, your culture, and your reputation from crashing.

The Reputation Line

A Defining Distinction in the DNA of Greatness

At the foundation of any reputation strategy lies the most important baseline you'll ever learn:

The Reputation Line.

This line is not theoretical fluff. It's real, it's practical, and it's powerful. It's the **line that protects or exposes**, that creates or destroys opportunity. It is **the measure of character in motion**— the invisible yet undeniable boundary that determines how others experience you and how you experience yourself.

How you choose to operate around this line determines your future.
Whether you're building trust or eroding it.
Whether you're earning loyalty or losing it.
Whether you're showing up as the person who builds legacies— or excuses.

The Distinction: Above or Below the Reputation Line.

The Reputation Line is simple to understand. But in practice? It's one of the hardest disciplines in life.

It defines the difference between:

- Blame and Ownership

- Excuses and Responsibility

- Denial and Accountability

- Justification and Growth

These are the behaviours that either elevate or erode your professional reputation. You can't have it both ways.

PROTECT/BUILD

RESULTS

OWNERSHIP

ACCOUNTABLE

RESPONSIBLE

REPUTATION

REASONS

BLAME

EXCUSES

DENIAL

JUSTIFY

RISK/DAMAGE

The diagram is deceptively simple. But it carries the **greatest leadership principle** I've ever worked with across thousands of people.

If you want to build a culture of greatness—**commit this
diagram to memory.**
If you want to lead a business others admire—**live above the
Reputation line.**
If you want to raise the standard for your career and your life—
own it every day.

Below the Line

Below the line are the behaviours that **damage, dilute, and
devalue reputation.**
You'll recognise them instantly—because they are the root of
everything that doesn't work:

- **Blame**

- **Excuses**

- **Denial**

- **Justification**

They sound like:

"That wasn't my fault."
"We've always done it this way."
"There wasn't time."
"I didn't know."
"It's someone else's job."

Here's the hard truth:
If you believe you don't dip below the line, you're already
there—**in denial.**
No one lives permanently above it. Not me. Not you. Not
anyone.

But the quality of your life and your leadership is directly proportional to **how long you stay below the line, before you take ownership and climb back up.**
That's the mastery.

Above the Line

Above the line lives everything great:

- **Responsibility**

- **Accountability**

- **Ownership**

Above the line is where reputations are built, trust is earned, and futures are created.
It's not just how you fix mistakes—it's how you operate, even when no one's watching.

If you look back at your proudest achievements, you'll find that **above-the-line behaviour was always present**.
Responsibility is the starting point.
You can't be accountable until you're responsible.
And you'll never take ownership without accountability.

That's the ladder of integrity.
That's what #1Reputation companies—and people—are made of.

Applying the Principle: The Test of Every Moment

Want to test this in your organisation?
Here's how.

When something doesn't go to plan—

Ask: **What behaviours were present?**
Look closely. Even if it seems unrelated, **dig deeper**—you'll find a below-the-line moment.
That's where the real learning lives.

And when you achieve something extraordinary—

Ask again: **What behaviours made it possible?**
You'll find consistency, ownership, and alignment.
Above the line. Every time.

The most successful cultures I've worked with—from billion-dollar businesses to small family-run teams—**all share this principle** at their core. They don't just talk about accountability; they live it, breathe it, and hire for it.

Make It Your DNA

The Reputation Line is not just a tool—it's a lens, a standard, and a mirror.

If you want to lead a team people want to follow …
If you want to build a business people trust …
If you want to be remembered for how you showed up in every room …

Make the Reputation Line your DNA.

Be the one who doesn't deflect.
Be the one who reflects.
Be the one who owns it—especially when it's hard.

Because that's the person who builds a #1Reputation— **And that person is you, if you choose.**

Beliefs → Reputation

Let's take it deeper.

One of the most **powerful forces in your culture** is something you don't always see—**Beliefs**.

Every individual on your team shows up with their own beliefs: about what matters, what's fair, what's worth their time, and how to deal with problems. These beliefs shape **mindset**, which in turn drives **attitude**—and ultimately produces the **behaviour** the market and team experiences. It's vital that we all understand that our reputations are moulded by our beliefs. The foundation of behaviour is rooted in an individual's beliefs in every moment.

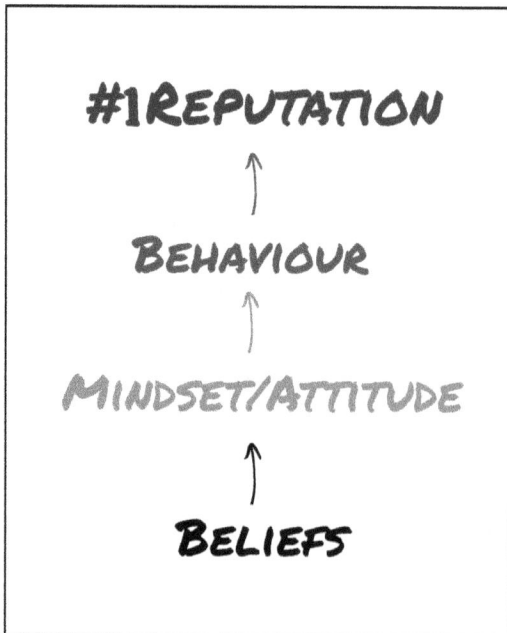

#1REPUTATION

↑

BEHAVIOUR

↑

MINDSET/ATTITUDE

↑

BELIEFS

The 3-Step Flow:

1. Beliefs → The invisible engine.

We all have them. They guide our worldview—on politics, religion, fairness, work ethic, customer care, and leadership. Your team may align on some—but never all. These are deeply ingrained and often unconscious. It's critical that you identify any limiting beliefs toward the company objectives and reputation. Especially in the front line CX team. When recruiting new team members, clarity of their beliefs must be understood during the interview phase. When on-boarding a strategic approach to induction and training must focus on identifying beliefs.

2. Mindset & Attitude → The filters we apply.

What you believe influences how you show up. A team member who believes "customers are annoying" will approach complaints very differently from one who believes "every complaint is a chance to win trust."

Poor customer experience = Poor belief system. Brilliant service = Strong belief in professionalism and care.

How does your team show up each day, do you have the attitude that predicts excellence or average?

3. Behaviour → The reputation reality.

This is the only part the world sees. Your team might *say* they care—but it's their **behaviour** that proves it. Customers judge your business by the actions of your people. As the saying goes,

Actions speak louder than words.

Reputation is the *measurement of behaviour over time*.

Here's the truth most leaders overlook:
You cannot change behaviour without changing beliefs.
And you cannot build a great reputation without addressing mindset.

Leadership – The Most Powerful Formula

The late, great **W. Edwards Deming**—the father of continuous improvement and quality management—defined one of the most profound yet underutilised leadership formulas of all time.

This formula applies as much to a frontline team leader as it does to a CEO of a billion-dollar enterprise. It also sits at the heart of companies that dominate their market with a **#1 Reputation**. We've adapted this principle into our research and analysis framework—because it shows up in *every piece of customer and employee feedback*. When the feedback is excellent, the foundations of this formula is always embedded and reflected in the actions of the team. When it's poor, one or more elements are missing. Without all three working together excellence is effectively impossible.

Deming's formula is as follows:

LEADERSHIP

THEORY
+
EXPERIENCE
+
PREDICTION

=

#1REPUTATION

<u>**Leadership**</u> Theory + Experience + Prediction = **Results** (Reputation)

At first glance, it seems deceptively simple. But the third component—**Prediction**—is where most leaders and companies fail. And it's why so few achieve true excellence in reputation.

Of every 1,000 people I've introduced this concept to—across keynotes, workshops, and boardroom sessions, I always ask what's the critical factor that starts with "P" —fewer than 20 can identify **prediction** as the critical missing piece. The common ones are: people, professionalism, performance, process, productivity, persistence, And yet, **prediction is the hinge upon which #1Reputations are built—or broken.**

Let's break it down:

1. Theory

This is your structure—your documented knowledge:

- Systems

- Processes

- SOPs

- Training materials

- Compliance frameworks

- Software platforms

- Strategy decks

It's what you *know* on paper. It's essential—but alone, it's not enough.

2. Experience

This is your *ability to act*. To execute.

- Can you bring theory to life?

- Do you know what real mastery looks like in motion?

- Can you lead through complexity, ambiguity, and pressure?

Experience bridges the gap between knowing and doing.

But here's the kicker …

3. Prediction

This is the rarest skill—and the ultimate differentiator.

Prediction is the ability to say: "Here's what we expect will happen—and here's how we'll respond if it doesn't."

Without prediction, theory and experience fall flat. Because without predictive capability, you cannot make credible promises. You can't forecast outcomes. You can't inspire belief or trust—because you're reactive, not proactive.

> *"Any statement devoid of a prediction is nothing more than information."*
> — *W. Edwards Deming*

This is one of the most important leadership truths you'll ever learn.

If you have theory and experience—but no ability to predict—you lack trust. You fail to meet expectations and your reputation suffers. In our customer and team experience interviews, when we trace dissatisfaction or underperformance, this is often the missing piece.

Prediction = Reputation in Action

Think of it like this:

- Theory is **credibility**

- Experience is **capability**

- Prediction is **accountability**

Reputation is built when you *predict* an outcome, *deliver* on it, and *own* it—publicly, consistently, and with clarity.

This is where most teams stumble. They issue vague timelines, ambiguous commitments, or generic promises. They aren't trained or empowered to make solid predictions, and they aren't coached on how to recover when a prediction fails.

Mastering **Theory + Experience + Prediction** doesn't just make you a better leader. It makes your company the most trusted, respected, and sought-after in your space. It creates a culture of integrity, performance, and excellence. It's the core driver behind #1Reputation—and it's in your hands to apply.

Here's what great leaders do:

When a prediction fails, they don't go below the line.

They don't blame the market, the team, or the supplier. Instead, they ask:

- "Where did we miss?"

- "Did we have the right theory?"

- "Did we have the right experience to execute?"

They use failure as **feedback**, not fuel for blame. This is how responsibility and learning cultures are built—one reflection at a time.

Where This Links to Your #1Reputation

At its core, **Prediction** is what ties your leadership model to your reputation model.

- **Customers** don't just judge you on what you say—they judge you on whether you do what you *said you would do*.

- **Teams** don't trust leaders based on charisma or vision— they trust those who say, "This is what we'll do," and then *deliver*.

- **Markets** don't value companies based on aspirations— they value those who fulfil their forecasts, targets, and values.

If you're not training your leaders to develop predictive thinking, you're missing the most critical part of performance, growth, and trust.

Leadership Scorecard for Reflection

Ask yourself and your executive team:

- Do we have the right **theory**? Are our processes, systems, and strategy truly best-in-class?

- Do we have the **experience**? Are our people skilled and prepared to execute under pressure?

- Do we make clear, confident **predictions**—and track them?

- When predictions fail, do we respond with ownership—or with excuses?

- Is **predictive thinking** part of our leadership development?

Leaders who master **Prediction** become the ones who shape markets, inspire loyalty, and earn reputations that precede them.

If you want a team that delivers at a #1R level, make sure they're not just trained in theory or seasoned by experience—but empowered to **predict, perform, and own the outcome**.

That's how powerful reputations are built.

The Only Two Mis-Takes in Business

There are only two real *mis-takes* in business. That's it. Just two.

Yet most people think mistakes are something to avoid at all costs. We've all seen it: team members afraid to speak up, managers burying errors, staff hesitating to take responsibility because they fear blame or backlash. And this is exactly the problem with cultures that focus on catching people doing things wrong.

When mistakes are seen as shameful or career-threatening, people stop growing. They stop learning. And your company slows down with them.

But here's the truth: **if you fear mistakes, you will never reach your potential.** Your best lessons come from the experience of getting it wrong—then doing it better.

As W. Edwards Deming said,

"If it's worth doing, then it's worth doing wrong for a little while."

That quote alone should be framed in every leadership office.

Change the Word. Change the Culture.

If you shift your mindset from *mistake* to *mis-take*—as in a misaligned action or a rehearsal, a take that didn't land—you unlock a new way of thinking. A mis-take simply means: you tried something and didn't get it quite right. Now you learn and try again. That's how real growth happens. That's how innovation happens.

Failing fast is not only more effective—it's far cheaper than failing slow.

I've tested this principle across teams in some of the most respected companies. It holds up 100% of the time. In cultures that embrace learning, not only does improvement increase, but *errors decrease*. Teams start thinking proactively. They solve problems before they escalate. They own their outcomes—and that's where transformation happens.

Like every principle in this book, this one isn't complicated. It doesn't require technical skills or theory-heavy frameworks. It just requires one thing:

The willingness to think.

Apply it consistently across your business, and you'll spark one of the most powerful shifts a team can experience: *a culture of responsibility.*

ONLY 2 MIS-TAKES

1. NOT ACT WHEN
   YOU SHOULD ACT

2. ACT WHEN YOU
   SHOULD NOT ACT

The 2 Mis-Takes

1. NOT ACT WHEN YOU SHOULD ACT

This is when something goes wrong because you didn't take action. You hesitated. You didn't follow up. You ignored a red flag. You avoided the conversation. You let the deadline slide. Whatever the reason—it didn't get done, and it mattered.

2. ACT WHEN YOU SHOULD NOT ACT

This is when the issue was caused because you jumped too early. You sent that email too fast. You gave the wrong instructions. You overpromised. You got involved when you shouldn't have. And things blew up.

It might sound *too* simple—but that's exactly why it works.

Almost every issue you'll face can be traced back to one of these two mis-takes. The goal isn't to blame—it's to clarify. Once you're clear on *which* mis-take occurred, you can focus on the fix.

Here's how to turn this into a leadership habit:

When You're Coaching Mis-Take #1

"So, you didn't act when you should have—how did that happen? And how can I help you so next time you know how and when to act?"

When You're Coaching Mis-Take #2

"So, you acted when you shouldn't have—how did that happen? And how can I help you so next time you know when *not* to act?"

Always Ask How, Not Why

This is a subtle but essential shift in language.

Asking **"Why?"** triggers defensiveness.
People go into justification, excuses, and self-protection mode.
This sends them below the line, fast.

Asking **"How?"** invites reflection.
It leads to thinking, learning, and forward momentum.

- "How did this happen?"

- "How could it have been different?"

- "How can we approach this next time?"

This is a game-changer for leadership conversations and cultural development.

These two mis-takes form the core of almost every challenge—and opportunity—you'll face as a leader or business owner. They give you a simple lens to view complexity. They give your team a safe, clear language for owning outcomes. And they give you a baseline to coach from without falling into *below the line* culture.

This is how you raise standards. This is how you develop critical thinkers. This is how you embed *above the line* responsibility into every layer of your company.

Because here's the truth:

- The teams that grow the fastest fail the fastest—and learn from it

- The leaders who build the best reputations make fewer mis-takes because they review them with clarity and responsibility

- The companies that reach #1R do so because their culture *knows* how to identify mis-takes early, correct them quickly, and learn constantly

Master these two distinctions—and you'll be mastering culture, performance, and reputation all at once.

Closing Thoughts:

The True Measure of Leadership

The *Generalised Principles of Greatness* are not just tools—they are transformative anchors for leadership, culture, and legacy. They aren't about systems, spreadsheets, or the latest technology. They are about people. About behaviour. About the belief that greatness is not random—it's created, consistently and consciously.

When you lead from these principles, you become more than a manager—you become a multiplier. A builder of belief. A cause of greatness in others. Teams don't just perform better; they become better. They don't just execute—they evolve. And that is where reputations are forged.

As Dr. John Demartini so powerfully said,

"Until we have a purpose greater than ourselves, we cannot expect to go beyond ourselves."

Far too many in leadership roles confuse authority with impact. The real leaders—the ones who are remembered—are those who lift others. Who see potential where others see limits. Who don't ask "What's in it for me?" but "How can I make it better for them?"

These principles form the backbone of enduring cultures and trusted reputations. If you already have a great culture, these ideas will elevate it to levels you didn't think possible. If your culture is fractured, this is your foundation to rebuild—stronger, clearer, and future-proofed.

Choose to be the leader who is remembered for helping others become their best.

Because at the end of the day—**Greatness Awaits.**

The only question is: are you willing to step up and lead it?

CHAPTER 9

A CHANGED WORLD DEMANDS A NEW STANDARD

#1

CHAPTER 9
A CHANGED WORLD DEMANDS A NEW STANDARD

The post-Covid business landscape is fundamentally different from the world we knew before 2020. In just a few years, we experienced a level of disruption not seen in decades—perhaps not in a generation.

Australia, in particular, enjoyed relative economic stability for over 30 years. Aside from a handful of key events—the early '90s recession, the dot-com crash, the Y2K scare, and the Global Financial Crisis—we've been the model of consistent, stable growth.

But between 2020 and 2022, everything changed.

The pandemic brought:

- Nationwide lockdowns

- Widespread work-from-home mandates

- Severe supply chain disruptions

- A surge in mental health challenges

- Shifting workplace dynamics

- The Great Resignation

- Historic labour shortages

- And now—soaring inflation

The world shifted dramatically, and business had to adapt—fast.

In the chaos, many companies dropped the ball. Amid all the operational chaos, **the customer experience (CX) suffered**. And now, the invoice is due.

The Decline in Service — And the Customer's Patience

Ask yourself:

As a consumer, how would you rate your experiences in the last few years compared to before Covid?

After asking thousands of individuals the same question, the data is clear:
Only about **10%** say customer service has improved post-Covid. The majority believe it's declined—and they're right.

Our research confirms this: service scores have **not returned** to pre-pandemic levels. And while customers were patient during the height of the pandemic, that patience has now worn thin.

In 2025, customers are no longer tolerating average. Inflation is biting hard, cost of living crisis and with every dollar spent, people are demanding **value and excellence**—not excuses.

The "Covid card" has expired.

Companies that fail to adapt will be left behind.

The Reputation Cost of Dropping Standards

For many businesses, the post-Covid era has embedded a new way of operating—one built around **lower standards, fewer touchpoints, and reduced effort**. For many it became their new standard of normal.

The critical danger?
This operating model is **no longer acceptable** to the market.

And yet, most companies are flying blind.
They don't know their current CX performance because they're relying on **internal opinions**, not **qualitative customer data**. Without customer insight, they're guessing—and guessing wrong.

If your team says the market is "tough," consider this:
Maybe the market isn't tough.
Maybe **you're not good enough**—yet.

The Cultural Hangover: The Danger of "Nice"

One of the most subtle yet damaging post-Covid trends is the rise of **NICE**—a behaviour that looks polite on the surface but masks a deeper cultural issue. We see signs in businesses about tolerance, and yes courtesy and patience are expected. The question is WHY do we need signs about behaviour, maybe some businesses have been ignoring the 'customer signs' that caused the need in the first place.

Let's break it down:

N.I.C.E. = Nothing Inside (me/us) Cares Enough

We've all experienced it:

- A bland meal that you describe as **"nice"**

- A haircut you don't love, but you say, **"It looks nice"**

- A new outfit that you don't care about but say **"that looks nice"**

- A customer interaction that feels hollow, even though the person smiled

NICE is the silent killer of customer experience.
It's smiling while saying no.
It's apologising without action.
It's surface-level courtesy without commitment.

In many companies today, CX is no longer a strategic priority.

- There's no CX lead

- No CX metrics

- No structured improvement plans

- CX only matters when there's a complaint

That's NICE in action.

And it's driving your customers away.

The Culture of No vs. the Culture of Yes

In a NICE culture:

- The team avoids hard conversations

- Promises are made but not owned

- "That's not my department" becomes a reflex

- No one feels responsible for reputation

But in a **#1R culture**, every challenge is an opportunity to serve. The standard response to difficulty isn't "no"—it's:

"How can we find a way to YES?"

Case Study: YES in Action

One of the construction companies I coach has redefined its reputation by building a culture around **avoiding "no" wherever possible**.

When customers say No —especially around pricing of certain features and options—they **listen**, take note, and stay agile. They avoid NICE.

Instead of closing the door, they keep it slightly open. Later in the project, when that feature or stage arises again, they revisit the conversation. In many cases, the customer's financial situation has changed, and what was once a no has now become a **YES**.

The impact?

- Customers feel seen and valued

- They get what they originally wanted

- The team builds deeper trust

- Reputation is powerfully enhanced—organically

And the proof is in the results:

- Their trophy cabinet is overflowing with CX and building industry awards

- Their customers become their advocates

- Their team continually innovates—just by asking, "What if we could?"

This is what a 10/10 culture looks like in real time:
Small improvements. Weekly reflection. Relentless progress.

Take the Leadership Challenge

Ask your leadership team:

"What are we doing to actively build and protect our reputation?"

If the answers are vague, defensive, or lack specific actions, then the **market will feel it too**.

Go deeper. Ask frontline staff:

- What are you protecting when you serve a customer?

- How do you handle a request that falls outside standard procedure?

- When was the last time you found a new way to say YES?

If you hear "We can't," "We don't," or "That's not our process," you've uncovered a core issue.

You're building **processes for efficiency**, not for **innovation**.

And the two don't always align.

Rebuilding Starts with Inquiry

So what can you do?

Start by being *unreasonable*.
Challenge every instance of "We don't do that."
Don't let the team settle into the comfort of average.

Ask yourself:

- Has our CX been diluted?

- Have we chosen easy over excellence?

- Have we become NICE?

There is no "easy" path to #1.
And there's no legacy in being NICE.

"Whatever it takes" is not a mantra—it's an **action**.

Redefine "Nice" as a Warning Sign

Integrate the NICE distinction into your management strategy. Remind your team that being polite without solving the problem is not service—it's avoidance.

True growth comes from being *unreasonable*.
Think of the people who shaped your career or your life. Were they always nice? Or did they challenge you to grow?

Being NICE may preserve harmony—but being direct, honest, and **solution-focused** builds strength.

Closing Thoughts:

Measure the Frequency of No

Track it. Audit it. Test it.

How often do your team members say "No" to customers?

And more importantly:

How many of those "No's" could have been re-engineered into a "Yes"?

Every reimagined No is an opportunity:

- To strengthen a system

- To empower a team

- To elevate your brand

- To build your **#1 Reputation**

And the best part?
It's the **team that finds the solution**—and **the team that earns the credit**.

It's no longer about avoiding failure.
It's about refusing to accept average.

The path to a #1R isn't NICE—it's bold, it's honest, and it's built on …

"how can we find a way to YES?"

CHAPTER 10

A FISH ROTS FROM THE HEAD FIRST

#1

CHAPTER 10
A FISH ROTS FROM THE HEAD FIRST

Does the Fish Really Rot from the Head First?

Whether or not it's biologically true, it is **absolutely true in business**.

I've seen it time and time again. Many of you have likely experienced it too: a new executive or manager enters the scene and immediately makes sweeping changes—**not** because they're necessary, but simply to make their mark.

It's ego at play. It's about asserting authority rather than serving the organisation. Unfortunately, companies often fall for this. Impressive interviews, polished resumes, and fudged references mask deep flaws, only to reveal chaos a year later.

When poor leadership takes the reigns, our research consistently shows a noticeable drop in customer experience (CX) and #1 Reputation (**#1R**) scores. Some insecure leaders even cancel our projects midstream—afraid of the market truth our independent data exposes. But the market always reveals the reality in the end, the market will always find the truth, it can't be conned for too long and it votes with its wallet.

What continues to baffle me is how people with little leadership capability still find their way into positions of influence, and I'm not just talking about government departments here; I'm talking about competitive, for-profit enterprises.

In contrast, the very best leaders I've worked with (and there have been hundreds at the highest levels) all share one critical trait: **they lead with data and facts first, not just theory or opinion.**

As W. Edwards Deming famously said:

> *"Without data, you're just another person with an opinion."*

We've all encountered leaders full of opinions, but when you ask them to back it up with their wallet—or their reputation—it's a different story. It's nothing more than **lipstick on the pig**.

Leadership Must Have a Higher Purpose

> *"Until we have a purpose bigger than ourselves, we cannot expect to go beyond ourselves."*
>
> *Dr. Jon Demartini*

Every leader in your business must view the company's reputation as **their highest priority**. Focus on #1R, and the rewards follow:

- Personal growth

- Professional credibility

- Enhanced team dynamics

- Loyal, valued customers
- Organic growth that secures jobs and opportunities
- Maxim profitability

When everyone aligns to #1R, **everyone wins**:

1. The team wins

2. The customer wins

3. The suppliers win

4. The business thrives

Of course, departmental KPIs remain critical. But it's essential to recognise how each KPI directly reflects your leadership and its contribution to #1R. If you're only aiming for *satisfaction*, you're setting the bar far too low. It's merely the starting line.

Satisfaction is the average of averages. It won't win awards. It won't create legendary customer loyalty, and it certainly won't build a powerful reputation. Satisfaction is a dangerous target because it breeds complacency. It's acceptable—but never exceptional. It's a trap as you end up irrelevant.

The companies with a true #1R aren't lucky. They are **designed** for it. It's the result of cultural alignment, clear process design, and a relentless pursuit of excellence. It's a powerful purpose from the heart to serve.

Leadership Sets the Ceiling

> *"No team can rise above the constraints of its leader."*

When leaders commit to building a #1R culture, they give their teams an extraordinary gift.

The best leaders empower their people to **build their own reputations**, seeing it as their most valuable professional asset. And when you help someone grow in their professional life, you help them grow in every aspect of life.

Think back to the greatest leaders and mentors in your own journey:

- They taught you how to think

- How to lead others

- How to see opportunities where others see obstacles

- How to identify risks—and solve them

- How to protect your integrity, no matter the circumstance

They left behind a voice in your head that still guides you today.

They warned of the cost of shortcuts.

They believed in doing it right the first time, knowing that:

> *"A quick fix is neither quick nor a fix."*

As a leader, reflect on your full scope of responsibility:

- Are you actively nurturing your team's engagement?

- Are you protecting your professional reputation and that of your company?

- Are you challenging yourself to go beyond task management and truly inspire?

I've witnessed young leaders embrace this mindset and skyrocket in their careers. They understand that their success is the direct result of **the success they inspire in others.**

The Decline of Leadership — And the Opportunity Before Us

It's no secret: **leadership is in decline.**

Look around—at businesses, governments, and society at large. So many distractions and lack of vision are impacting purpose and inspiration. The widening gaps, rising costs of living, and social unrest all trace back to one root cause: poor leadership.

Leadership is, and always has been, the solution.

What happens when ego runs unchecked?

- Manipulation

- Coercion

- Culture erosion

- Self-infatuation

And inevitably, the best people leave, while the mediocre remain. Study after study confirms: **people don't leave companieshey leave poor leadership.**

In *Chapter 8: The Generalised Principles*, we unpacked the proven foundations of effective leadership. Make sure you deeply understand them. They will define not only your leadership style but your legacy.

There has never been a better time to lead.
When most businesses settle for average, it's **easier than ever to stand out.**

When things are tough, go harder.
In tough times, true champions rise.

Sport Mirrors Business: Everyone Wins Together

> *"When it comes to being #1, there is no finish line."*
>
> *Darrell Hardidge*

Sport offers a perfect metaphor for company culture.

Championship teams understand:

- Every role matters

- The person cutting the oranges matters just as much as the star player

- Victories belong to everyone

How does your organisation celebrate success?

- When sales lands a big contract, is it celebrated company-wide?

- Does the entire team feel part of the victory?

- Is the positive impact on the company explained at all levels

Sadly, many companies fall into silos.
The front-line team becomes disconnected from the back office.
Wins become isolated, and culture fractures.

In great organisations, **a win is a win for all.**

Ego destroys culture.

Check it at the door.

Case Study: From Blame to Breakthrough

We once delivered a customer feedback program for a complex, high-value construction product. The initial findings were grim:

- Poor communication

- Misalignment across departments

- Frustration from customers

In the executive debrief, one manager immediately tried to blame others:

"Let's guess which clown stuffed up this project."

This was a classic **below-the-line reaction**.

But our data told a different story:

- Sales and production teams were not aligned

- Communication breakdowns were rampant

- Internal respect and understanding were missing

We introduced a powerful exercise: **"A Day in the Life."**

- Salespeople spent time on the factory floor, learning production realities

- Factory workers shadowed the sales team, understanding customer pressures

- Project managers swapped roles with sales and the factory team

- Marketing went on sales calls and onsite

The transformation was extraordinary.

Factory teams gained empathy for the daily hustle of sales. Sales teams learned to manage customer expectations realistically. Both sides developed **mutual respect** and built collaborative workflows.

Project management understood the challenges from sales to factory.

Six months later:

- Customer complaints vanished

- Communication became a customer-highlighted strength

- Margins improved due to reduced rework and smoother production

- Factory teams visited job sites, saw their work in action, and took pride in their contribution

This is the magic of **aligned leadership and culture**.

Closing Thoughts:

Inspire Greatness from Within

As a leader, ask yourself:

- How can you inspire extraordinary improvements within your team?

- How can you empower them to design better CX processes?

- How can you help them see their role in building and protecting reputation?

When teams understand the challenges, they become the best architects of the solutions.

When you align them to a shared purpose, they don't just comply—they **create**.

Leadership is the catalyst.

Your reputation is the outcome.

Greatness awaits.

CHAPTER 11

10/10 IS A MINDSET, IT'S NOT A CHECKLIST

#1

CHAPTER 11
10/10 IS A MINDSET, IT'S NOT A CHECKLIST

Culture is the breakfast of champions.

And it's true. For high-performing teams, the pursuit of greatness is as essential as their morning meal. Delivering a 10/10 experience isn't just a goal—it's a way of life. It's an obsession with excellence and a relentless defence of your #1 Reputation (**#1R**).

As we explored in a previous chapter, 10/10 is not the result of a single action done perfectly. It's the result of **100 small actions, done consistently at 1% better every day.** Culture is the compounding effect of behaviours—each reinforcing the next. The behaviour is the result of the mindset and the mindset is the result of beliefs.

As a leader, you are the conductor of this orchestra. You set the tempo. You lead the harmony. Without alignment, your team will sound like squealing cats—what should be a symphony becomes chaos.

Ask yourself:

- How do you set up each day, week, or month for your team?

- Are they left to their own devices, or aligned under a common purpose?

- How do you know they're match-fit and ready to perform?

- How do you measure 1% improvements?

10/10 Is a Mindset, Not a Checklist

Too often, companies confuse procedures with culture.

When asked about their approach to service excellence, they refer to their manuals, flowcharts, and checklists. And while these are useful tools for guidance, **they are not guarantees of excellence.**

As I've outlined in the chapter on *The Generalised Principles*, the formula:

Be x Do = Have is absolutely critical here.

You can "do" the checklist with mediocrity.

- You can follow procedures with a tired mindset

- You can be friendly without truly smiling

- You can listen without actually hearing

- You can pretend to care and be of service

The checklist alone will never deliver a 10/10 experience. It's not just about **what** you **do**—it's about **who** you are **being** while you **do** it.

The mindset behind the action is everything.

10/10 requires a deeply embedded belief system and it can never be assumed that a person has it:

> *"In this moment, my responsibility is to deliver the best possible experience with my skill and effort with the greatest intention."*

This takes focus.

It takes training.

It takes commitment.

And, importantly, it takes time.

But not everyone will naturally have this mindset.

And it certainly doesn't happen by accident.

Guarding Against the False Sense of Success

One of the biggest risks is the team believing that **checking the boxes equals excellence.**

Checklists confirm tasks were completed—but they don't guarantee how they were delivered. Without the right mindset, you may be delivering all the tasks but providing an average (satisfactory) experience.

To build a true 10/10 culture, you must **challenge the beliefs behind the behaviour.**

Ask your team:

- What does 10/10 service mean to you?

- Why does it matter and what's at stake?

- How do you approach different customer situations?

- What beliefs guide your service delivery?

- Who's responsible for customer loyalty?

- What's in it for you?

Whether it's a face-to-face conversation, a phone call, an email, tech support, warehouse handling, or delivery—it doesn't matter. The same principles apply. Service excellence is driven by the mindset behind the action.

Most companies settle for **satisfaction**—because they don't know any better. The don't understand the game behind the game.

Just look at the marketing out there:

- *"Customer Satisfaction Guaranteed."*

- *"Our customers are highly satisfied."*

- *"5 Star Satisfaction rating"*

But satisfaction is average. In effect you're irrelevant.
Satisfaction is survival, not success.
If your target is satisfaction, you are guaranteed mediocrity.

10/10 is not "as good as it gets."
It is **beyond that.** It is *brilliance* and it is *transformational.*

As a leader, you must know how to:

- Inspire and cause it

- Measure it

- Train it

- Hold your team accountable to it

Excellence Must Be Predictable

If you want a #1R, your team's behaviour must be predictable.

Excellence is not random. It's not hit and miss. It must be baked into your operational DNA. This requires hard work, time, patience, and relentless focus.

Most importantly, **leaders must model it in every interaction—** internally and externally.

You cannot expect excellence in customer experience if you tolerate mediocrity in team experience. If internal culture is average, external CX will reflect that.

The mindset of excellence is what separates extraordinary companies from average ones.

In your business:

- What is the required mindset?

- What does 10/10 look like at every touchpoint?

Whether you're providing professional services, selling products, or handling logistics, you need precision at every stage. You need a team that checks the boxes **and** delivers with passion, attention, and care.

Lessons from My Own Team

In my own business, when we ran projects of high-volume customer experience interviews of over 8000 customers, I invested heavily in **team mindset before performance.**

Each morning, we would check in on our call team.

My call centre manager had a sharp instinct—she could sense when someone wasn't quite in the right headspace. If they weren't fully present, they wouldn't deliver exceptional experiences on the phone.

Rather than push them, we had a policy:

- Take a break and go for a walk

- Clear your head

- Move to admin tasks if needed

- What will it take for you to be present in the moment and focused

I respected my team immensely for this honesty. Some would come in and say:

"Today's not my day. I've had a rough morning."

We never saw this as weakness.

We saw it as professional responsibility.

Because if they weren't at their best, it would affect our reputation. And we valued our #1R too much to risk it.

This taught us a powerful lesson:

Mindset isn't optional—it's the foundation of excellence.

Building a culture of YES

To truly create a culture of excellence, your team must think **beyond themselves**.

In *Chapter 9: The Distinction of NICE*, we explored how avoiding NO and striving for YES is transformative. This is where your team's mindset powers your competitive edge.

Finding a way to YES is hard work.

- It's disruptive.

- It requires innovation.

- It demands collaboration.

- It's going beyond yourself

But this is where breakthroughs happen.

Every time your team pushes past default answers and genuinely seeks solutions, they strengthen your reputation. Customers notice. They remember.

And they return.

> *"Whatever it takes is an action—not a theory."*
>
> *Bill Allen*

When your culture embodies this, you create a market-leading point of difference.

A company that relentlessly seeks ways to say YES becomes a company that customers—and team members—stay extremely loyal to.

Closing Thoughts:

Greatness is not born from routine.
It is born from relentless intent to improve.

Build your checklist for excellence but empower it with a 10/10 mindset. Make it your standard operating procedure to expect brilliance from every role, every person, every interaction. Ensure the clarity of understanding that Satisfaction is the average of averages.

Audit every touchpoint between your team and your customer. Measure. Train. Adjust. Refine.

And most importantly, **lead by example**.

Understand that Motivation always requires external pressure to act.

Whereas Inspiration is a powerful force from within.

If you want your team to deliver 10/10 service, give them a 10/10 leader.

Then, watch how far they can go.

CHAPTER 12

THE CASE FOR THE CHIEF REPUTATION OFFICER

CHAPTER 12
THE CASE FOR THE CHIEF REPUTATION OFFICER

Who's Responsible for guarding the #1 Asset?

As I've worked through end-to-end assessments of CX and Reputation, one insight has become undeniable: Most organisations, regardless of size, have a critical structural gap. And this gap quietly undermines their ability to truly build and protect their most valuable asset: their **reputation**.

I understand the natural resistance to introducing yet another role into an already busy structure. No leader is eager to add more responsibility to their agenda. However, when designed and staffed correctly, this role pays exponential dividends.

It's not a role for just anyone.
It requires a unique mindset and a very specialised skill set.
Ideally, you already have the right person in your team—someone who lives and breathes your culture and is ready for their next step.

The role I have identified and created the structure for is the **Chief Reputation Officer (CRO)**.

The CRO: The Guardian of Reputation

The CRO is not an administrative function.
They are not a desk-bound observer. The individual requires a unique approach to the role and requires experience that reflects their knowledge of business operations.

The CRO is the living, breathing connective tissue between departments, linking every role back to the company's ultimate goal: to protect and elevate its reputation. They hold the golden chalice of the company and they ensure the **Reputation Covenant** is ever present.

They report directly to the CEO or the People & Culture leader, acting as both an advisor and an enabler. One of their critical responsibilities is to support the People & Culture function, especially when it comes to team assessment and the direct relationship between internal culture and customer experience.

Too often, department heads underestimate their impact on CX and #1R.

- **CFOs** may assume CX is irrelevant to them—until invoicing errors tank customer trust

- **Warehouse managers** might think their job is purely operational—until dispatch errors destroy customer confidence

- **Procurement teams** may dismiss CX concerns—until poor stock planning leads to shortages and customer frustration

Every single department impacts the customer experience. Every team member is part of the reputation machine.

The CRO ensures they understand this—clearly.

They work side by side with People & Culture to embed this understanding across the business.

The CRO Is in the Field, Not behind a Desk

This is not a passive role.
The CRO integrates deeply with all teams, asking the tough, necessary questions:

- *Is this process enhancing our reputation or placing it at risk?*

- *Do our teams have what they need to deliver excellence?*

- *How is the onboarding of new managers progressing?*

*Do we need to act decisively with this customer situation?*Their focus extends to employee engagement, ensuring that there is:

- A structured employer-of-choice strategy

- Regular engagement metrics

- Appropriate training and support

- Clear understanding of what's at stake in protecting the company's reputation

The same applies externally: the CRO monitors CX metrics and customer sentiment, ensuring there's no disconnect between internal culture and market perception.

Aligning Leadership and Breaking Silos

Supporting leadership teams to perform at their best has always been a challenge. Every department has different priorities. Every manager fights for budget. Egos and politics are unavoidable.

But data tells the story:
Leadership alignment directly impacts CX and reputation.
And yet, many companies don't see it—because they lack **real customer data.** What they think they know isn't so.

Fragmented leadership creates fragmented service.
Department goals become more important than shared goals, leading to turf wars, misalignment, and a dilution of service excellence.

This is where the CRO brings coherence.
The CRO removes the silos and instils a unified focus on CX excellence and #1R.
They make sure no one forgets what the ultimate goal is—regardless of role or title.

They also become the voice for those high-integrity team members who might otherwise be drowned out by louder, more political agendas.

For People & Culture leaders, the CRO is an invaluable ally. They provide clear, honest reports on company culture, based on real engagement data and real customer insights.

Who Owns Reputation?

One of the most fascinating patterns I've observed is this:
In every CX and Reputation project we've delivered, when
results are outstanding, **everyone** claims the credit.
But when the results are poor?
The finger-pointing begins.

This is the danger of distributed responsibility:
When reputation is everyone's job, it often becomes no one's job.

The CRO **prevents this dilution**.

They own the feedback loop. They ensure clarity and accountability
across every department. They make sure the insights from team
and customer feedback are not just collected—but acted upon.

Here's the reality:

- The CEO is too stretched

- The GM is overloaded

- Sales, Marketing, and Operations already have full plates

The CRO fills this critical gap, ensuring that customer and culture
insights are **never pushed into the "later" pile**.

Through fast check-ins, regular reporting, and proactive
conversations, the CRO keeps leaders aligned and focused on
what matters most: **reputation health**.

The Single Most Valuable Asset

Your reputation is not an abstract concept.
It's your company's single most valuable asset.
It's controlled by your team and decided by the market.

The CRO ensures every team member understands:

- What they are protecting

- How they contribute to reputation

- Why it matters every single day

Through structured feedback loops, they integrate customer insights and team sentiment to maintain full organisational alignment.

The CRO is not a luxury.
They are a necessity.

In a fragmented world of shifting markets, heightened customer expectations, and increasing competition, **the CRO is the leader you never knew you were missing.**

Closing Thought:

The role of the Chief Reputation Officer is not just about preserving reputation—it's about building a future where reputation becomes your greatest competitive advantage.

If you're serious about building and maintaining a #1 Reputation, this is the role that will get you there.

Greatness Awaits

Further information if considering this role.

Chief Reputation Officer (CRO) – Role Description Template

Position Title:
Chief Reputation Officer (CRO)

Reports to:
CEO / Head of People & Culture

Purpose of Role:

The CRO is responsible for the continuous protection, improvement, and management of the company's most valuable asset—its reputation. Acting as the connective tissue across all departments, the CRO ensures alignment between internal culture and external customer experience, driving organisational excellence towards #1 Reputation (#**1R**) status.

Key Responsibilities:

- **Company-Wide Reputation Stewardship**

    o   Embed #1R principles across all departments
    o   Ensure every team member understands their role in protecting and elevating the company's reputation

- **Internal Culture Alignment**

    o   Partner with People & Culture to maintain a highly engaged, reputation-focused team

    o   Monitor team engagement metrics and onboarding processes

- **Customer Experience Management**

  o Ensure customer feedback loops are in place and research insights are acted upon

  o Collaborate with customer service and operational teams to resolve CX gaps

- **Leadership Support**

  o Assist department heads in aligning operational goals with reputation outcomes

  o Facilitate cross-departmental communication to prevent silos and fragmentation

- **Risk Management**

  o Identify reputational risks early and work proactively to mitigate them

- Review processes regularly to ensure they align with the company's reputation goals **Reporting & Accountability**

  o Provide monthly reports to the CEO and leadership team on internal engagement, CX performance, and reputational health.

  o Deliver actionable insights from customer and employee feedback

Ideal Skills & Attributes:

- Exceptional cross-functional leadership
- Strong understanding of customer experience and organisational culture

- Proactive, solutions-oriented mindset
- Excellent communicator and relationship builder
- Analytical, data-driven decision making
- High emotional intelligence (EQ)
- Unwavering commitment to integrity and the company's values
- Clarity of the full business cycle from marketing to final market delivery

Success Indicators:

- Improved CX metrics and customer retention
- High employee engagement scores
- Fewer internal silos and stronger collaboration
- Proactive risk identification and resolution
- Elevated market perception of the brand
- Clear alignment between internal culture and external experience
- Improved efficiency directly linked to internal communication

CRO Appointment Checklist

Use this checklist when appointing and onboarding your Chief Reputation Officer.

Preparation

- Define the CRO role in the leadership structure
- Secure CEO and leadership alignment

- Clarify reporting lines and expectations

- Identify internal candidate(s) who exemplify company values and culture

- Prepare communication plan to announce role internally

Appointment

- Formally appoint CRO and share job description

- Announce to the entire organisation, highlighting purpose and goals

- Provide onboarding briefings with:

  o People & Culture

  o Customer Service

  o Department Heads

  o Marketing / Brand team

Setup Systems & Support

- Establish regular leadership team meetings with CRO reporting

- Grant access to customer feedback systems and employee engagement data

- Equip with tools for data collection and reporting

- Define internal reputation risk flags and response protocols

Early Wins

- CRO conducts initial company-wide reputation audit

- Deliver first "state of reputation" report to leadership

- Establish quick-win projects (cross-departmental alignment, CX improvements)

Ongoing Development

- Quarterly reputation health check

- Monthly reporting cadence

- Provide CRO with continuous leadership development

- Celebrate wins and recognise progress regularly

Here is a quick quiz for you:

Chief Reputation Officer Knowledge Test

Are you leading reputation — or leaving it to chance?

Instructions:

Answer honestly. There are no "safe" answers here. This test is designed to reveal assumption gaps and areas where your reputation may already be at risk.

1. Ownership & Accountability

Who in your organisation is explicitly responsible for measuring and protecting your reputation?

- ☐ CEO
- ☐ Marketing
- ☐ CX/Service
- ☐ HR/People & Culture
- ☐ Nobody

Describe how they measure it (beyond financials or NPS):

2. Departmental Impact

List how each department affects reputation (positively or negatively).

- Finance:_____
- Procurement: _____
- Warehousing/Logistics:_____
- Sales/Marketing:_____
- People & Culture: _____

Do you currently measure these impacts? ☐ Yes ☐ No

3. Predictability vs. Assumption

Of your top 20% of customers (who deliver 80% of revenue):

- % you know are at **10/10 appreciation**: _____
- % you believe are safe but haven't measured: _____
- % at risk (below 9/10): _____

How confident are you? ☐ 100% ☐ Somewhat ☐ Guessing

4. CRO Role Definition

If you created a Chief Reputation Officer role tomorrow:

- What 3 things would they do differently from CX, HR, or Marketing?

1. _____
2. _____
3. _____

5. Reputation Risk Awareness

When was the last time your executive team received a structured "reputation risk" report (covering CX, TX, supplier alignment, and market trust—not just NPS)?

☐ Within the last 3 months
☐ 6–12 months ago
☐ Over a year ago
☐ Never

If never: what risks could already be hidden in your business?

Scoring Insight

- If most of your answers rely on *assumptions*, you're exposed

- If your reputation is measured only by *opinions, NPS, or financials*, you're blind to real risk

- If you don't have a CRO—or a leadership equivalent— you're missing a vital strategic role

A #1Reputation isn't built on assumptions. It's built on data, clarity, and leadership.

CHAPTER 13

THE GREAT ASSUMPTION TRAP

#1

CHAPTER 13
THE GREAT ASSUMPTION TRAP

There's a dangerous assumption that silently undermines many companies.

It goes something like this:

> *"We're busy, the order book is full, the cash is flowing, complaints are few, and the frontline team reports everything is good. So, our reputation must be fine."*

This, however, is not a fact—it's an opinion.

As W. Edwards Deming famously said,

> *"Without data, you're just another person with an opinion."*

When it comes to your company's reputation—arguably your most valuable asset—you cannot afford to rely on assumption or internal sentiment alone. Yet, this is the exact trap that catches many organisations off guard. They have little or no data on CX to challenge any assumptions of the leadership team.

When Assumptions Collapse

Every business has experienced it: a seemingly loyal, high-value customer suddenly defects to a competitor.
When asked why, management typically offers opinions:

- *"They slashed prices."*

- *"A new manager switched to a friend's business."*

- *"Head office made the decision — it was out of our hands."*

While these might explain the surface, rarely do they tell the whole story.
The truth is usually deeper, tied to gaps in execution, culture, or customer experience that leadership has overlooked.

Most businesses place heavy focus on acquiring new customers, with sales teams promising the market that they are the best choice. However, it's the **entire operational engine**—not just sales—that delivers (or fails to deliver) on that promise. The reality is the sales team set up the new customer with an ideal fit/solution and then handover to the rest of the team. Are they set up for success from a precise handover process, or is it left to an assumption they will be well cared for?

What's worse: companies often lose their best customers and immediately turn their focus to replacements, never truly understanding why they lost them in the first place. Consider the cost of replacement, often it's a long period before the financial break-even occurs, and then you are only back to zero balance, no gain, no loss, just replacement.

Data vs. Assumptions: What the Numbers Show

Our research reveals a sobering truth.
Satisfied customers, on average, demonstrate only **48% loyalty**.

Even when customers seem happy, they still buy from your competitors. Most businesses assume they have their fair share of the customer's wallet, but in reality, they often fall far short. This is where the measurement of satisfaction causes the assumption of loyalty, its superficial loyalty its far from unshakable loyalty.

When we ask customers directly about their purchasing habits, the results are eye-opening.
There's frequently a wide gap between perceived wallet share and actual wallet share.

The goal should always be 100% of your customer's wallet—being their **only supplier**.
But this is earned, not assumed.

A score of **9 or 10 out of 10** in customer experience secures this loyalty. Anything below that leaves the door open for competitors. Here's how it typically breaks down:

The Reputation Score Breakdown

- **10/10: Most Trusted Supplier**
  You are the go-to provider. Trust is at its peak, and customers value you as irreplaceable.

- **9/10: Strong Promoter**
  Close to perfect. These customers are loyal advocates, helping to grow your reputation.

- **8/10: Satisfied but Vulnerable**
  "Fine" but not exceptional. You're meeting expectations, but you're not their only choice. At this level you must observe the competition. Risk exists.

- **7/10: Reputation at Risk**
  This score signals concern. Customers may be actively considering alternatives. Satisfaction is merely just OK, loyalty at this level is at 25%.

- **6/10: Damage Control Zone**
  Loyalty is extremely weak. Customers tolerate you mainly due to convenience or price. They have alternatives and you're a transaction.

- **5–0/10: Reputation Breakdown**
  High risk. If given an option, these customers would already be gone—and they're likely spreading negative word of mouth. The opportunity for increased wallet share is non-existent.

The Critical 70% Rule

Your top-tier customers—typically the 20% that generate 80% of your revenue—must be safe and secure.
If fewer than **70%** of these critical customers score you a 9 or 10, your revenue and reputation are exposed to significant risk.

That means nearly **1 in 3 of your best customers** may be sitting in the danger zone of 8/10 or lower. Replacing a customer at this level is extremely challenging, and the impact on revenue and margin can be serious.

A question to reflect on:

If you never lost a customer, how many new customers could your business truly handle?

It's astonishing how many companies accept customer churn as inevitable, without truly understanding the reasons behind it. If churn is happening, and it's not because of external, unavoidable factors, then it's happening due to service or price gaps.

Accepting churn without analysis is complacency at best—and costly negligence at worst. Poor leaders increase pressure on marketing and sales teams for a quick fix rather than find the root cause.

The Danger of Underestimating Low Scores

One of the most concerning trends we see is leadership teams underestimating low customer scores.
For example, in a recent client project, 21% of their top clients rated them below 7/10.
That's over **1 in 5 key customers unhappy**—yet management dismissed it as non-critical because revenue targets were still being hit.

This is dangerously short-term thinking.
When markets tighten, as they inevitably do, companies in this position get exposed.
The damage to professional reputation is already done—it just hasn't shown up in the P&L yet.

Action Steps to Eliminate Assumptions

Here's how to safeguard your company against dangerous assumptions and secure your reputation:

1. Implement Precision Measurement

Your CX measurement system must be rigorous, clear, and based on a 10-point scale.
Vague satisfaction ratings (like *"satisfied, somewhat satisfied"*) **tell you nothing**.
Go deeper.
Get to the *why* behind the score.
Online surveys alone won't cut it—you need proactive, qualitative, professional feedback.

2. Continuous Feedback Loops

Regularly engage your team about customer experience and service levels.
Empower them to spot risks and suggest improvements.
Issues ignored will fester. Involve your team in testing and refining your CX process. When they build it, they own it.

3. Never Rely Solely on Revenue Data

Revenue is a lag indicator.
You must balance financial performance with real-time customer sentiment data.
Challenge internal assumptions relentlessly. Just because money is coming in today doesn't mean your reputation is secure tomorrow.

4. Act on Low Scores Aggressively

Treat customers rating you below an 8/10 as urgent priorities. Understand their concerns and build specific action plans to lift them into the safe zone of 9 or 10. Proactive recovery not only saves accounts but often builds greater loyalty than a flawless experience.

Closing Thoughts:

The most dangerous thing you can do as a leader is assuming your reputation is safe because the numbers look good on paper. Most reputational damage is invisible—until it's too late.

Ask yourself and your leadership team:

"Are we operating on facts, or assumptions?"

Challenge complacency.
Demand data.

And remember: your reputation isn't defined by internal opinion—it's defined by your customers actions.

Ensure you're not falling into the great assumption trap.

Visual tool for leadership teams to spot customer risk instantly.

How to Use:

- List your top revenue-generating customers (80/20 rule applies)

- Record their latest CX score (1–10)

- Categorise them by risk level (Safe / At Risk / High Risk)

- Prioritise actions based on risk severity

Customer Name	Revenue Value ($)	Latest CX Score (1–10)	Risk Level	Action Priority	Notes
ABC Corp	$1,200,000	9/10	Safe	Monitor	Loyal promoter
XYZ Ltd	$850,000	7/10	At Risk	Immediate follow-up	Address service gaps
LMN Group	$2,500,000	6/10	High Risk	Critical action	Executive outreach required
DEF Pty Ltd	$400,000	8/10	Borderline	Improvement plan	Increase engagement
GHI Inc	$1,000,000	5/10	High Risk	Crisis response	Investigate root cause

Quarterly conversation framework to challenge assumptions and surface hidden risks.

When to Use:

- Quarterly leadership team meetings

- Executive retreats

- Special risk reviews

Discussion Prompts:

Customer Risk & Assumptions

- *What assumptions are we currently making about customer loyalty?*

- *Who are our top customers scoring below 8/10, and why?*

- *What's the "silent churn" we might not be seeing?*

Data & Decision Making

- *Are we relying too heavily on revenue numbers instead of customer sentiment?*

- *What feedback loops need to be strengthened?*

- *Which customer complaints feel like "noise" but might actually be signals of deeper issues?*

Leadership Accountability

- *Do all department heads understand their role in reputation protection?*

- *Who owns the response to at-risk customer feedback?*

- *Are we quick enough in acting on CX risks?*

Action Planning

- *What proactive strategies can we implement before issues arise?*

- *Where can we increase internal collaboration to reduce risk?*

- *Who are our internal "Reputation Champions" to recognise this quarter?*

CHAPTER 14

#1REPUTATION AUDIT

CHAPTER 14
#1REPUTATION AUDIT

As I've been designing and implementing this new process and measurement for #1R, it became clear that creating an audit for businesses to self-assess was essential. Because if you don't know what questions to ask, how will you know where you really stand?

The Reputation Audit is a series of carefully designed questions that challenge you to search for the answers—truthfully.

There is a self-scoring process to this, and in this chapter, you'll find a QR code linking to the audit on our website, where you can complete the process and be sent your #1R Report and Insights.

There are two essential audits:

- **Internal**: The Team and Culture Audit
- **External**: The Market Reputation Audit

#1R Team and Culture Audit

First rule: Be honest.
There's no benefit in kidding yourself.
If nothing changes, then nothing changes—where you're at is simply where you're at.

Treat this as an opportunity to learn, improve, and ultimately transform.

The reputation audit for your team should always involve your People and Culture Manager or HR leadership.
This is critical—especially given the significant changes in team dynamics over the last few years.
New employees bring their past experiences with them, and whether you realise it or not, they impact your culture.

One key distinction: **knowing what to do is not enough.**
Checking the right boxes in recruitment is not enough. Someone may have ten years of "experience," but if they've been trained to operate at an 8/10 standard—where "near enough is good enough"—then that's the mindset and behaviour you inherit. And **that** will limit your ability to build a #1R company.

Your audit must assess more than skills.
You must measure **attitude**—the mindset behind the behaviour.
If your people have yet to be trained to think like a #1, you must determine whether it's coachable—or not.
Not everyone will make it.

You also need to assess the **psychometric fit** for each role. Square pegs in round holes won't build your future. Your HR and People & Culture teams must be equipped to protect both the functional and emotional alignment of your organisation.

Another critical reflection point:
How does your team feel about the company's future?
Is there optimism? Is there belief? Is there energy?

Certain industries are feeling nervousness in the current economy. A brilliant businessman once told me:

"If the economy shrinks by 3%, economists call it a disaster. But there's still 97 cents on every dollar out there. Go harder and get it."

If the market shrinks, **be better than everyone else**.
Be so good that customers fleeing average competitors **run straight to you**.

> **"Different isn't always better, but better is always different"**

From the great Marshall Thurber

The best people want to work for the companies with the best reputations.
Your reputation as an employer is not a side project—it's a strategic asset.
Audit it ruthlessly.

Market Reputation Audit

Your external audit focuses on **revenue** and **customer dynamics**—the lifeblood of your business.

This audit must be completed by:

- Sales and marketing teams

- General managers

- Key department heads tied to revenue

- And importantly, the back-end teams who support frontline delivery

Your internal customers (your team) are critical in supporting your external customers (your market).
Both must align—or your reputation fractures.

This audit will test the team's **knowledge**, **assumptions**, and **depth of experience** with the market.
Have each department head complete it independently, then compare answers.
Variations will **reveal misalignments**—and open up strategic conversations that must happen.

Your aim is to uncover:

• Where you are aligned with your vision of a #1R

• Where you are at risk

• Where urgent action is required

The insights will be eye-opening.
In many companies, managers set new revenue targets with the best intentions—but the rest of the team lacks the clarity and tools to deliver.

Often, your Financial Controller fights a lonely battle, chasing cash flow and margins while the sales team isn't trained and educated to leverage the Compounding Reputation Formula (see chapter 16). Meanwhile, the operations team often has little awareness of their impact on customer experience.

Remember:
Your sales team brings customers through the front gate. But your entire organisation must keep them happy in the paddock—and slam shut the back gate to prevent customer churn.

Customer churn is your #1 risk factor.
Drill deep to understand **why** a customer leaves, not just **when** they leave.

Why This Audit Is Different

The #1Reputation Audit is a new concept—and I don't believe there's anything else quite like it.
It's been built from our **real-world, in-the-trenches data**:

- Hundreds of thousands of customer interviews
- Hundreds of companies across multiple industries
- 16+ years of learning what actually moves the needle on reputation and performance

Most customer experience audits are shallow, automated, or rely on biased internal feedback.

This audit cuts straight to the truth—because your company's future demands it.

Take your time.
Answer honestly.
Review your insights.
Then get to work.

The Ultimate Question

When you finish your audits, step back and ask:

If I were buying my own company today, would I pay a premium for its reputation—or ask for a discount?

Your answer will tell you everything you need to know.

Now, let's build something that commands a premium.

Go to www.1reputation.net/audit to do your #1Reputation audit.

CHAPTER 15

TEST, MEASURE & MASTER YOUR REPUTATION

#1

CHAPTER 15
TEST, MEASURE & MASTER YOUR REPUTATION

What you don't measure you can't manage

Testing and measuring are the foundation of high-performing businesses. Without them, your organisation is flying blind. While most companies track financial performance, compliance, or safety depending on their industry, very few have a robust measurement strategy for the two most critical indicators of long-term success: **Customer Experience (CX)** and **Reputation**.

The Blind Spot in Business: Measuring Reputation

Many companies assume their reputation is solid because:

- Revenue is coming in.

- Complaints are minimal.

- The team says "things are fine."

But this is assumption, not insight. And assumption is dangerous.

If your reputation is your most valuable asset — and it is — then it must be *measured*, *monitored*, and *protected* like any other strategic asset. If you were to ask your team what the most valuable asset of the company is, would they mention Reputation? If not, then you have a major gap in understanding this critical fact.

Beyond Revenue: What Are You Actually Measuring?

To build and protect a #1 Reputation (#1R), you need to know:

- Are we delivering consistent 10/10 experiences?

- Do we really understand what 10/10 actually means for our market?

- Are the team leaders clear on the foundations of 10/10 and communicating and empowering effectively?

- Are we measuring the performance of departments, sales, product delivery, and support — wherever revenue and relationships are influenced?

- Are we as a company 10/10 to work for?

Most businesses can't answer these with confidence.

Financials are the rearview mirror. You need **real-time insights** into how your market *feels* about your business and how your team *represents* your brand. Without the metrics it relies upon a lot of guesswork and luck. You may have the unique experience in the team but relying upon that alone is risky. You must know how to measure the critical factors in your reputation.

What You MUST Test and Measure for #1R.

1. Customer Experience (CX) Metrics

High-Quality CX Scoring

You need deep, qualitative feedback—not shallow surveys. Focus on interviews or direct contact methods to uncover emotion, trust, and unmet needs. Analysis is critical. Satisfaction metrics cannot measure excellence; you must use a 0-10 scoring format.

Retention Rate (Correlated to Score)

Understand what percentage of your market scores you 9 or 10 out of 10 and continues to buy. This ratio creates massive leverage when aligned with revenue. The scores below 9 have a direct relationship to lost revenue and sale value.

Referral Rate

What percentage of your customers risk their own reputation to refer you? Referrals from 10/10 customers are gold — they come with no marketing cost and high conversion. Measure who refers, what they refer, and what those referred customers are worth. Knowing that 10/10 customers refer 6 times more than 8/10 customers ensure you have the reason and the financial return to invest in the best feedback process.

Value for Money

Your value perception must align with the experience. If CX scores drop, people start measuring value based on the invoice instead of the outcome. That's the path to price pressure and commoditisation. You must know what creates your value driven economy and link it to service experience.

Support & Responsiveness

How well do you help customers when they need something difficult or time-sensitive? Do you have a reputation for "whatever it takes?" Do your team members make high-value suggestions? Do they have a reputation for understanding customer needs? Helpful, proactive service is one of the greatest contributors to trust.

Trust Score

Trust must be actively measured. Without it, #1R is impossible. Low trust often comes from unresolved issues, unkept promises, or dismissive behaviour. Map this against CX data for clarity. Do you know what the key drivers of trust are in your business?

2. Team Experience (TX) Metrics

Your team owns and controls your reputation. If your internal experience is average, your external reputation can't be exceptional. Are you the employer of choice?

Culture Feedback (Real Feedback)

Most "culture surveys" fail. Why? Because team members don't trust them. They're vague, anonymous, and rarely acted upon and they are reactive. How can you probe into responses and beliefs if you aren't in control of the feedback in real time. You need an environment of safety where people can share honest feedback without fear of retribution.

We only use **confidential phone-based Team Experience (TX) interviews**, never online surveys. Why? Because the truth is personal. And truth builds transformation. Clarity of the truth ensures your authenticity when dealing with issues.

Retention Score

Ask your team:

- *Will you still be here in 12 months?*

- *Would you refer a friend to work here?*

- *How do you feel about your manager?*

- *What's your Sunday night feeling about Monday morning?*

Culture is emotion. And emotion predicts commitment.

Career Alignment

- Are people clear on their development pathways?

- Do they feel supported when they ask for help?

- Is there regular, proactive career guidance?

If people aren't progressing, they're regressing. Or leaving.

Team Clarity on Reputation

Does every team member know what the company's reputation is—and what role they play in protecting it? Can they explain how they contribute to a 10/10 experience? If they can't, then you have results based on very diverse individual beliefs around what excellence is.

3. Integrated Reputation Metrics: CX + TX

Your customer experience scores mean little if your team is burnt out or disengaged. And you'll never achieve 10/10 CX with a team that's running on fumes. You must have an inspired team, not a team that requires motivation.

You must measure both CX and TX together.
Without this, your insights are only half the picture. Together they provide clarity and understanding of your two critical pillars of reputation.

The Cost of Not Measuring

We've worked with companies shocked to lose top-tier clients. Their assumptions were wrong. They thought they had loyalty, when in reality, they only had **satisfaction** — and satisfaction is fragile.

Worse still, some businesses dismiss poor scores altogether. They place their own opinions above the experiences of their customers, creating a re-active culture impacting the front-line teams ability to serve.

Build Your Reputation Scorecard

1. **CX Metrics**
   o   % of clients scoring 9–10
   o   Referral volume and value
   o   Retention rates linked to experience scores
   o   Communication how do you rate as a company
   o   Understanding customers specific needs and business operations scores
   o   Response time to support requests
   o   Perceived value-for-money
   o   Trust scores linked to referral and retention

2. **TX Metrics**
   o   Retention rate and future intent
   o   % of team who'd refer you as an employer
   o   Sentiment around leadership and career growth
   o   Direct connection between role and company reputation
   o   Are you the most trusted employer

3. **Reputation Integration**
   o   Weekly CX/TX leadership pulse check
   o   Departmental score accountability
   o   Monthly "Reputation Risk" briefing
   o   Chief Reputation Officer monthly overview

Closing Thoughts:

You Can't Improve What You Don't Measure

The most successful companies don't leave reputation to chance. They **measure it**, they **own it**, and they **build it** from the inside out.

If you're not actively testing and measuring CX and TX, your business is vulnerable.
If your leaders assume satisfaction equals safety, your revenue is at risk.
If your team doesn't understand their role in protecting your reputation, culture will drift.

Are you assuming the strength of your most valuable asset?

Now is the time to build your customised test and measure strategy.
Design it. Run it. Refine it.
And watch your reputation rise to #1R.

CHAPTER 16

THE COMPOUNDING POWER OF A #1REPUTATION

CHAPTER 16
THE COMPOUNDING POWER OF A #1REPUTATION

4 Powerful Steps to predictable growth

To build a business with a #1 Reputation (#1R), you must master the four revenue drivers that form the foundation of predictable, scalable growth. These four pillars determine how your revenue is generated — and when combined with an exceptional reputation, they deliver exponential results.

The formula is simple:
Leads × Conversion Rate = Customers
Customers × Frequency × Average Sale Value = Revenue

A company with a #1R multiplies this formula by maximising every variable. They know their numbers across all four pillars and as discussed in the previous chapter they have mastered Test & Measure.

Understanding the Reputation Revenue Model

Here's how it works:

1. **Leads**
   Customers who are referred to you by a trusted source convert faster, spend more, and stay longer. A strong reputation drives high-quality lead flow. Remember 10/10 experience scores refer 6 times more than 8/10 (satisfied).

2. **Conversion Rate**
   Buyers who trust you are already primed to say yes. Your sales process becomes less about convincing and more about aligning. Your referrers have done all the hard work for you.

3. **Frequency of Transactions**
   Delighted customers see you as their preferred supplier, they come back more often — for every relevant product or service you offer.

4. **Average Sale Value**
   A strong relationship allows you to offer more — and upsell without friction. Clients want to buy more from those they trust.

This is the **Compounding Reputation Formula**:
Small gains in each area lead to powerful, sustainable growth — all driven by your reputation. Business at this level seems almost effortless, it's the most efficient, and the most profitable.

The Multiplier Effect of 10% Gains

Let's run the numbers as an example over a year. If you:

- Increase leads by 10%

- Improve your conversion rate by 10%

- Boost transaction frequency by 10%

- Increase average sale value by 10%

  Your revenue grows by **46%**.

Reputation Formula	Yearly	10% Increase	5% Increase
Leads	4000	4400	4200
Conversion Rate	25%	27.50%	26.25
Customers	**1000**	**1210**	**1103**
Average Sale value	1000	1100	1050
Transaction frequency	2	2.2	2.1
Revenue	**2,000,000**	**2,928,200**	**2,432,115**
Revenue Increase		**46%**	**21.6%**

Even a modest **5% improvement across the board results in 21.6% growth**.

That's the power of compounding. And it starts with how your customers *feel* about you. Anyone who thinks going the extra mile doesn't pay, don't understand.

"without data your just another person with an opinion"

Why Most Companies Miss This Opportunity

Most businesses fail to track these metrics in detail. Instead, they focus on:

- Expensive marketing strategies

- Generalised brand awareness

- Reactive service and basic satisfaction scores

- The deals the competition are doing

Meanwhile, the greatest untapped asset sits right in front of them:

The existing customer base.

When someone buys your business, they're not buying your logo. They're buying your relationships, your reputation. Your customers are the engine — and how they feel about you determines your future.

Training Your Frontline to Leverage #1R

The missing link in many businesses?
Professional, reputation-aligned sales training.

Your frontline team — salespeople, account managers, BDMs — are the face of your brand. They must understand:

- How the compounding formula works

- Their responsibility in each revenue driver

- How to sell from a position of trust and value

- How to leverage a #1R

And most importantly: **How to protect the company's reputation** in every interaction.

You must train them to a **10/10 standard**. Otherwise, you're leaving opportunity — and revenue — on the table.

In Chapter 19: *How to Sell Your #1R*, we break down the exact sales process that aligns with this model. But at its core, your team needs to **measure and report** their performance across these areas. That's where coaching, improvement, and accountability live.

Are you training your front line in these principals and strategies?

Data Over Opinions: What the Numbers Reveal

In our research, we ask customers:

- In the next 12 months is your business growing?

- Will that growth require more of our products or services?

- Would you like someone to contact you?

In many industries, **60–70% of customers say they're growing, and 80% of them welcome additional support from their supplier to manage the growth**.

Most companies never uncover this. Why?
Because their teams aren't trained to ask and most don't understand their customers business.
They're reactive, waiting for orders, instead of proactively serving and guiding their customers.

The result?
Untapped demand. Missed sales. Lost loyalty. Inviting competition.

What's extraordinary, mostly when we deliver these insights the sales management and team are surprised. I then explain the compounding revenue formula and their customers growth statistics and question their current sales growth target.

If you have a 10-15% growth target, then maybe you don't have the clarity of what business already exists in your customer base?

Measuring What Matters

If you want to activate your compounding reputation formula, start tracking these metrics across your sales team:

1.   **Lead Source Breakdown**

     o   Where are leads coming from? What's their conversion rate?

2.   **Sales Conversion Rate**

     o   Per rep, per product, per market segment.

3.   **Transaction Frequency**

     o   How often are customers buying? Where's the opportunity to increase?

4.   **Average Sale Value**

     o   What's being offered? Are there add-ons, upgrades, or complementary products being missed?

Compare these across sales teams/account managers. You'll often find quiet champions — people delivering exceptional results simply by serving better, building trust, and being proactive.

The Magic of Account Management

When you combine a strong reputation with world-class account management, something extraordinary happens:

•   Customers trust you enough to tell you what they really need

- You're able to recommend what's best for them — not just what you sell

- You generate high-margin revenue with almost no acquisition cost

- You cause the cycle to start over again

Every sale becomes easier. Every referral becomes warmer. Every interaction strengthens the bond.

Referrals Are the Highest-Value Leads

The best kind of business is one that walks through the door *because someone else said you're the best.*

That's why referrals are the most powerful proof of a #1R.

But here's the key:
You don't just earn referrals by being "good".
You earn them by delivering experiences that make customers **feel** they're in safe hands. That's what makes them willing to stake their own reputation on you.

And when someone refers you, treat that referral with the highest integrity. If you're not the best fit, **educate them honestly**. The referrer will still look good — and your reputation grows.

Most Companies Undervalue the 4 Pillars

Here's what we commonly see:

- No lead source tracking

- No conversion analysis per rep

- No system to increase purchase frequency

- No process to improve average sale value

But they still spend heavily on ads, campaigns, and promotions. Bringing leads in the front gate and leaving the back gate open.

Want powerful, profitable growth?
Work the relationships you already have.

Your current customer base is **your greatest revenue engine** — and your #1 tool to strengthen your reputation. Consider the effort and expense going into new customer acquisition, and imagine if 50% was invested in sales training, CX research and retention strategy.

Final Actions for Implementation

1. Train your frontline in the Compounding Reputation Formula

2. Set KPIs across all 4 revenue pillars

3. Ensure your CRM or reporting tools capture this data

4. Conduct regular account reviews focused on growth, not just retention

5. Tie performance to CX scores — especially 10/10 loyalty indicators

6. Don't settle for 10% growth targets when the formula allows for 20–40%+

The Compounding Reputation Formula Toolbox

A fillable workbook template with sections to calculate:

- Monthly leads & conversion rates

- Number of customers & frequency

- Average sale values

- Forecasted revenue increase with 5%, 10%, 20% improvements

Salesperson Performance Tracker

Per team member:

- Lead source origin

- Conversion %

- Frequency of interaction with existing accounts

- Average invoice value

- Referral tracking

- CX score linkage (customer feedback)

Sales Coaching Questions Sheet

Prompts for sales leaders to use in 1:1s or team huddles:

- "What's your highest-converting lead source?"

- "How can we increase conversion rate without discounting?"

- "Where can we increase frequency?"

- "Which clients are not buying everything we can offer?"

Account Growth Strategy Template

To map proactive conversations with existing clients:

- Future needs

- Cross-sell opportunities

- Referral potential

- Loyalty check-in questions

Role-Play Scripts & Language Templates

- How to ask for referrals authentically

- How to explore needs without sounding "salesy"

- How to explain value (not price)

Closing Thoughts:

When markets slow, most companies panic. But the best don't blame the economy — they **examine their own excellence**.

Is the market tough, or are we just not good enough to have a #1R?

When your team is trained, your data is clear, and your reputation is strong, growth isn't a theory — it's the natural outcome of doing the right things, the right way.

Build your business around your reputation.
Train your people to protect it.
Measure what matters.
And let the numbers — and your customers — lead you to the top.

CHAPTER 17

THE REPUTATION INDEX FOR THE #1 ERA

CHAPTER 17
THE REPUTATION INDEX FOR THE #1 ERA

The State of Play in CX Measurement

The Net Promoter Score (NPS) revolutionised how businesses measure customer experience (CX) and loyalty. It was a groundbreaking shift—simple, effective, and easy to implement. Its core concept was elegant: ask your customers how likely they are to recommend you to others. A high score indicated advocacy. A low score exposed a lack of trust.

And for years, it worked.

It gave companies a snapshot of their standing with customers and helped track loyalty trends. But as with most once-novel ideas, overuse, misapplication, and commodification have diluted its value. Today, companies rely heavily on automated surveys, generic metrics, and vanity numbers—often without understanding what they truly mean.

Customers are tired. They're bombarded with surveys, star ratings, follow-up requests via text, email, apps, and receipts. It's no longer valuable—it's intrusive. CX has become another checkbox exercise in many organisations. And with this fatigue, the real risk is that **businesses are making critical decisions based on flawed or surface-level data.**

Here's the uncomfortable truth: **many companies are flying blind.**

They assume if revenue is stable, they must be doing fine. If complaints are low, all is well. If frontline feedback sounds good, reputation must be strong. But as **W. Edwards Deming** famously said:

"Without data, you're just another person with an opinion."

And if you're only relying on internal opinions or generic survey tools to gauge your market reputation, you're placing your **most valuable asset—your reputation—at risk.**

When NPS Isn't Enough

While NPS has its place—particularly in high-volume B2C markets like retail, hospitality, and personal services—it struggles to capture the full complexity of B2B relationships or high-value transactions. Why?

Because the B2B world moves differently. Decisions are bigger. Risks are higher. Switching costs are greater. One lost customer can mean millions in revenue, while one new client might take 12 months of relationship-building to secure.

With such a high gradient of investment Vs risk, you absolutely cannot use a generic email survey tool to get the critical feedback from your highly valuable customers. Besides all else its almost disrespectful.

"You are so important to us as customer; however, we will only spend small change in research programs to find out if we are delivering on our promise and if our team are taking great care of you".

Did you know it's approx. 15% that complete online surveys, so the data is skewed and inaccurate. The silence from the majority leaves you to guess.

Would you risk your relationship with a high value customer, to save money on quality research? Unfortunately, that's what most of the market does, spends huge to get a new customer and virtually $0 keeping them.

There is no strategy for retention if there is no customer research.

"Hope is not a strategy"

Winston Churchill

In these markets, two critical concepts are often ignored:

1. Lag Time

Customers may not leave even if they're unhappy. They may stay because the transition is too hard. Systems, contracts, timing, relationships—all play a role. This "lag" creates a false sense of security. Many companies believe their customers are loyal, when in reality, they're **just not ready to leave—yet.**

2. Complexity

Customer experience in B2B is not a single transaction—it's a journey with multiple stakeholders, service interactions, and expectations. Many survey tools don't account for this complexity. They reduce nuanced relationships to a single number and assume that score tells the full story. It doesn't.

The Birth of a New Metric: The Reputation Index

With these shortcomings in mind, I spent the last 15 years working on a better way to measure **true reputation**—beyond satisfaction, beyond surface metrics, and beyond NPS. After **over half a million phone-based interviews**, we created a new standard. This is an overview, the IP is unique, and its application specialised. The following provides an insight to the metric:

The Reputation Index.

This metric goes deeper, measuring the **true depth of customer sentiment, trust, loyalty, and advocacy.** It was developed specifically for:

- High-value B2B relationships

- B2C businesses with high emotional or financial investment

- Organisations with multiple touchpoints or long-term contracts

- Franchises, Dealerships and multiple locations

- Companies looking to measure both external reputation and internal team culture

The Reputation Index provides a **composite score out of 5**, built from **six interrelated pillars**, each weighted to reflect the dynamics of modern reputation-building.

The Six Pillars of the Reputation Index

1. Customer Experience Score

How would the customer rate their overall experience doing business with you? A simple 0–10 scale, much like the original NPS—but contextualised and part of a broader framework with deeper analysis.

2. Likelihood to Return

Not just how they feel now—but how likely are they to **actually return**? This is a strong indicator of future cash flow, and essential for forecasting.

3. Referrals Given

Have they actually referred you? Not just "would they," but **did they risk their own reputation** by recommending you to someone else? This is one of the most powerful forms of trust and loyalty.

4. Issue Management

When they had a problem or needed help, how well did your team respond? Did they feel supported? Were they heard, helped, and guided toward resolution?

5. Proactive Recommendations

Have your team made suggestions to help customers get the best from your products or services? This measures insight, understanding their business model, and your alignment with the customer's success.

6. Trust

Do they believe you operate in their best interest? Are you transparent, honest, and consistent in your dealings? This pillar captures the emotional and ethical foundation of your relationship.

Scoring the Reputation Index

Each of these pillars is scored and weighted to create a composite Reputation Index score out of 5. The thresholds are as follows:

Index Score: 5 — #1R Most Trusted

You are the most trusted and respected brand in your market.

- 80%+ of customers rate you 9 or 10 across all areas

- You are their first choice and often, their only choice

- Referrals and loyalty are high. Churn is extremely low

Index Score: 4 — High Performer

You have a strong reputation, but there's room to grow.

- High levels of customer appreciation (9 & 10) scores

- Many in the range of 8/10—where the wow factor may be missing

- Referral rates and proactive engagement need improvement

- A focused plan could elevate you to #1R

Index Score: 3 — Mid-Range Some Risk

You're holding steady—but vulnerable.

- 50% of customers rate you 9 or 10, 35-40% are satisfied rate you 7 or 8, 10-15% are detractors below 7/10 and at risk

- Loyalty is okay but not locked in. Churn is happening

- In the price trap with high need for customer acquisition

- There's inconsistency in CX delivery across departments

- Competition is active in your market

- You have the experience in the team for excellence, but it will require a different structure to what you have around training

Index Score: 2 — At Risk

You're operating under false assumptions.

- Most customers are between 7 and 8/10. Just meeting expectations

- Your 7/10 customers are you highest risk as they are one negative experience away from being a detractor and ready to move

- Up to 20% may be detractors (0-6). Effectively 1 in 5 are unhappy and this will cause major expense to rectify the issues. Profits are low and new customer acquisition is high and very expensive

- Referral rates are low. Trust is wavering. Service is reactive, not proactive

Index Score: 1 — In Decline High Risk

You are in damage control.

- High churn, low trust, inconsistent service

- Majority of customers score you 7 or below

- Loyalty is driven by price or convenience, not value or trust

- Customers are demanding with low engagement

- Staff morale and team reputation are likely poor as well

- Re-engineering of the business is critical to survive and be profitable

The above scorecard provides a very clear insight into the behaviours within the business. If you have an exceptional culture, it will be reflected with a high index score, the opposite also occurs.

Measuring Internal Culture: The Internal Reputation Index

External reputation and internal culture are connected.

You can't deliver a 10/10 customer experience with a 7/10 team experience.

That's why we created an **Internal Reputation Index** using the same framework. We measure:

- Whether your team would recommend you as an employer

- Whether they trust leadership

- Whether they feel supported, challenged, and developed

- Whether they understand their role in protecting the company's reputation

- Do they believe in the company's mission and purpose

When you combine the external and internal Reputation Indexes, you gain visibility across **both sides of the customer journey**. It becomes a strategic tool for:

- Leadership alignment

- Team development

- Culture building

- Growth planning

- Risk management

Why Most CX Programs Fail

In recent years, I've sat in dozens of meetings with CX managers, marketing directors, and even CEOs who proudly show me their survey tools and NPS dashboards.

But when I ask simple questions—like:

- What's your referral ratio by segment?

- What's your retention ratio by segment?

- What percentage of your 80:20 clients are at risk?

- What percentage of customers actually rate you #1R?

- What's your customer churn cost?

- What does customer acquisition cost?

- What are the critical touchpoint scores in the customer journey?

- What are the behaviours behind 10/10 excellence?

- What are the head and heart drivers of CX?

—very few can answer.

Even worse, many confuse marketing activity with CX performance. They're tracking page views and ad spend but **not understanding why clients stay or leave.**

This is the great disconnect: businesses are investing in growth while **leaving retention and relationship management to chance.**

The Cost of Not Knowing

If your business has 80% of revenue tied to 20% of clients, then those clients are your most critical asset.

Yet very few companies measure:

- How many of those clients would refer you

- How many feel "just satisfied" (8/10)

- How many are drifting toward competitors

- Which internal departments are driving loyalty—or causing risk

You cannot afford to assume everything is fine because revenue is steady. Many companies have experienced the **shock of a key customer suddenly leaving,** and the reasons—price, preference, timing—are often **symptoms, not causes**.

If you don't dig deep, it will happen again.

Why the Reputation Index Matters Now More Than Ever

In the post-COVID world, customer expectations have changed. Patience is thin. Loyalty must be earned every day.

Your **CX process needs to evolve**, especially if you're in high-value, relationship-driven markets.

The **Reputation Index** isn't a replacement for NPS—it's an evolution. It's built for the complexity of high value relationships, and it allows you to:

- Identify where trust is breaking down

- See who your real advocates are

- Align internal behaviours with customer expectations

- Protect revenue and margin through insight, not guesswork

Your Next Step

If you're serious about building a #1R company—one known as the **most trusted in your category**—then you must **measure what matters.**

Ask your leadership team:

- What's our current Reputation Index score?

- Which departments are affecting it most?

- How aligned is our internal team on reputation ownership?

- Who is responsible for improving it?

- What's the plan?

This isn't just CX. This is **your future market position.**

Closing Thoughts:

Reputation is the currency of trust.

And in a world of disruption, trust is the most bankable asset of all.

Move beyond assumptions. Move beyond surface surveys. Measure what matters. Lead with integrity.
And build a company your market—and your team—can be proud of.

The Reputation Index is not optional. It's essential

CHAPTER 18

THE POWER OF LEVERAGE

#1

CHAPTER 18
THE POWER OF LEVERAGE

Mastering the Multiplier Effect of #1R

The Distinction of Leverage

Leverage, in its purest form, is the ability to achieve **ever more with ever less**.

When you've built a **#1R (#1 Reputation)** in your market, you've earned the right to leverage the hard work, consistency, and trust you've invested in. A #1R is not just a badge of honour; it's a **business asset** that can and must be **strategically deployed** for growth.

Leverage is not about working harder. It's about **working smarter**—amplifying the return on your existing relationships, processes, team alignment, and customer and supplier partnerships. It's about making everything easier, more efficient, and more impactful—**because of your reputation**.

The Compounding Effect of Reputation

Leveraging your #1R produces a **compounding effect** when done correctly. The momentum builds across three key stakeholder groups:

1. Your **team**

2. Your **suppliers**

3. Your **customers**

When these three forces are in alignment—operating synergistically with a mindset of 1% improvement per week—you create a flywheel of performance. The sum of incremental gains produces exponential outcomes over time. The impact on reputation is organic and secure.

Let's explore how to unlock this leverage inside your business.

1. Leverage from Within: The Team Multiplier

The first area of focus is **your internal team**. As discussed in detail in Part 2. They are the guardians of your reputation. They own the customer relationships, the supplier communication, and the day-to-day decision-making that defines your brand. Challenge them to think beyond what they know today. To **re-imagine** what's possible.

Your team needs to **see themselves as reputation builders**. This is especially important in the account management, operations, and delivery functions. Ask them:

- Where are the untapped opportunities?

- Which customers and suppliers already trust us deeply?

- Where can we gain speed, efficiency, or exclusivity by better aligning?

- If we were to grow 20% where would our challenges be?

- Where do we need to adjust our process for growth?

You'll be surprised how many hidden opportunities exist when you **proactively assess your network**—especially with your suppliers.

2. The Untapped Opportunity in Supplier Leverage

Too often, companies fail to realise the strategic value of being the **#1 customer** to their suppliers. When your business is respected and easy to work with—when you pay on time, communicate clearly, and show loyalty—your suppliers will go out of their way to support you. How do you know, because that's what you do for your #1 customers.

"Cheap means late. Value means on time."

This principle is especially powerful in industries where product availability, quality control, or service delivery are highly dependent on third-party suppliers.

Let's look at a practical example.

Case Study: Strategic Leverage in Construction Supply Chains

A construction business dealing with hundreds of projects and thousands of supply transactions sat down to map their supply chain. They asked:

- Who are our top 10 suppliers?
- Who are the key account managers or contacts we work with?
- What are our shared frustrations?
- Where can we improve workflow, predictability, and performance?
- What would 10/10 communication look like?

In one instance, they identified a long-time supplier whose products they loved—but who was consistently slow in providing quotes. This delay was impacting their ability to get pricing to customers and close deals. There were situations where they lost sales due to delay.

The company scheduled a meeting and shared the **real-world consequences** of these delays. The supplier was shocked—they had no idea the impact was so severe. In response, they co-designed a **priority rating system**:

- **Category 1**: Urgent — top of the list, immediate action

- **Category 2**: Medium — 24–48 hour turnaround

- **Category 3**: Low — next available window

This small innovation dramatically improved quote turnaround time, built mutual respect, and **deepened the partnership**. Communication immediately improved beyond any standard before. The big impact, they were now winning sales due to speed of quoting. Everyone wins.

Proactive Supply Collaboration During Uncertain Times

During the Covid-era, supply chains were volatile. One steel company proactively worked with suppliers to forecast needs, place forward orders, and even **secure inventory with prepayment or holding fees.**

This ensured that when competitors were scrambling, they were delivering on time—building trust, reliability, and a reputation for excellence.

"If you're a supplier's favourite customer, they will prioritise you—because they respect you."

And remember: **being #1 doesn't mean being the biggest.** It means being the most valued and respected.

3. The Power of Customer Leverage

Now, shift your focus to your **customer base**.

You've likely got clients who **absolutely love working with you**—those who've referred you, advocated for you, and made your business better. But are you **intentionally leveraging** these relationships?

Ask yourself:

- Do our account managers know which clients hold us in the highest regard?
- Are they proactively engaging these clients about upcoming projects, supply needs, or partnership opportunities?
- Have we locked in future business through exclusive arrangements or priority access?

Sitting down with your top clients—even just 30% of your base that considers you #1—can unlock **future revenue, forward planning, and competitive protection.**

Leveraging Through Proactivity

When your team sits with a client and asks:

- "What's happening in your business over the next 3–6 months?"
- "Is there anything we can prepare for in advance?"
- "Would you like to pre-order or reserve stock?"
- "Can we offer guaranteed supply or priority pricing?"

You move from being a vendor to a **strategic partner.**

Your competitors won't even know the opportunity exists—because **you've already locked it down.**

How to Build a System of Leverage

To truly master leverage, you must design it into your operational rhythm. Here's how:

Map Your Leverage Points

- Who are your top 10 supplier contacts?

- Who are your top 10 customer advocates?

- What are their priorities, frustrations, and growth plans?

Collaborative Planning

- Schedule regular reviews with key partners (suppliers & customers)

- Share forecasts, needs, and challenges

- Co-create systems that benefit both parties

Empower Your Team

- Train account managers in strategic communication

- Ensure they understand the compounding revenue formula

- Teach them how to identify and activate leverage

- Hold them accountable for maintaining strong relationships

Measure Leverage Outcomes

- How much future business is locked in?

- How often are pre-purchase orders used?

- Are your suppliers proactively supporting you?

- Have lead times shortened or efficiency improved?

Why Most Businesses Miss This Opportunity

The problem is **everyone's busy**. Fires are being put out daily. People are in reactive mode. The bandwidth for strategic supplier and customer planning often doesn't exist—unless it's intentionally carved out.

But the truth is this: **leverage is one of your most profitable, untapped assets.**

- It shortens the sales cycle

- It reduces stress and rework

- It improves forecasting and cash flow

- It creates predictable customer experiences

- And most of all, it enhances and protects your #1R

The Final Frontier: Total System Leverage

Mastering leverage across your **team**, **suppliers**, and **customers** transforms your business from a collection of departments into a unified force.

It allows you to:

- Plan future cash flow with accuracy

- Pull deposits forward

- Secure supply in a volatile market

- Reduce churn and increase lifetime value

- Create **unshakable customer loyalty**

Even if you currently hold a #1R with only 30% of your client base, your focus should be **expanding that zone**. Work strategically to increase the share of customers who see you as irreplaceable.

Measure it using the **Reputation Index**. Track improvement over time. Monitor internal and external indicators. Get feedback. And use the insights to keep building.

Key Reflection Questions

- Where in your **supplier network** are the hidden leverage opportunities?

- Who in your **customer base** sees you as a vital part of their success?

- How do your **account managers** engage in strategic planning with clients?

- Are your team members trained to communicate and collaborate with leverage in mind?

- Do your current systems encourage proactivity or reactive firefighting?

Closing Thoughts:

Profit Is in the Leverage

The final layer of the #**1R strategy** is **leverage**. It's where you move from hard work to smart growth. It's where you turn trust into predictability, partnership into performance, and goodwill into results.

You've spent years building relationships.
Now it's time to make them **work for you**.

Leverage is not luck.

It's a mindset. A system. A discipline.
Master it, and you will unlock the next level of sustainable growth, reduced stress, and market leadership.

You already have what you need—
You just need to activate it.

CHAPTER 19

HOW TO SELL YOUR #1R

CHAPTER 19
HOW TO SELL YOUR #1R

Everyone's in Sales When You're building a #1R

One of the most powerful and untapped leverage points in any business is achieving a #1R **for service excellence**—and making it your point of difference in the sales process. When you're known for delivering exceptional service, **your reputation becomes your sales engine**. It becomes the credibility behind every promise you make and the proof behind every word your team says.

Your **sales process is your covenant in action**. It's your company saying, "This is who we are, and we deliver on our word." But here's the truth: **everyone on your team is in sales**. Not all will agree with that—or even realise it—but it's reality.

So ask yourself:
What do they say when asked about where they work?
How do they describe their job, their company, their leadership?
What do they say when someone asks, "Are they good to deal with?"

Because whatever they say—**that's your sales message**.

This is where **Team Experience (TX)** becomes mission-critical. If your TX is low, it's almost certain they're not out there talking about how much they love their job or how proud they are of your product or service. They're not selling—they're silently repelling potential customers.

True sales success begins with alignment. It begins when your team is proud to represent your company and supports your reputation with consistency.

And the gold? **Referrals.** When customers risk their own reputation to refer you, it's the highest trust. Understanding *why* they do—and measuring it—gives you a scalable sales strategy rooted in integrity.

This chapter is written with the insight from a trusted colleague: Martin Eade—one of the best sales trainers in the market. His wisdom has helped shape world-class sales cultures, and Martin unpacks how leaders can optimise their sales teams by anchoring everything to the foundation of **reputation**. Sales is a prized professional skill.

I knew a chapter was needed to clarify the critical essentials in sales process, while it's just a quick look over the fence, it defines the need to build a #1 sales team and sales process.

Let's hear from Martin.

Reputation – The Real Currency of Sales

Let's have a serious conversation.

Not about sales techniques. Not scripts. Not conversion funnels.

Let's talk about the one thing that drives *everything else* in sales … and in business.

Reputation.

Now I want you to picture this—your product, your business, and your salespeople are all aligned. They're not just "good"—

they're *trusted*. Your clients don't shop around. Your price is never questioned. You don't chase leads—they chase you.

That's what reputation delivers.

This chapter is about **why** reputation is the real currency of sales, **how** to build it at every layer, and **what** happens when you get it wrong—or right.

The Reputation Trifecta

There are three reputations in every sale. Miss one, and you bleed revenue. Nail all three? You become unstoppable.

1. **The reputation of the product**

2. **The reputation of the salesperson**

3. **The reputation of the business**

Let's unpack each one.

1. Product Reputation – "Does This Thing Work?"

This is the foundation. The bedrock. If the product doesn't deliver—none of the other two matter. You might sell it once, maybe twice, but long-term? You'll burn.

We've all bought lemons.

And we never forget.

A poor product reputation sticks. It travels fast and deep. But here's the thing—**even a great business can't overcome a bad product forever**.

You know this already.

Even premium brands have flops. Apple's "antenna-gate," Coca-Cola's "New Coke," Mercedes recalls. But these companies survived. Why?

Because they fixed it. Fast.

They *ran* toward the problem. And in doing so, they reinforced trust.

Because that's the key to product reputation—it's not about perfection.

It's about **how you respond when things go wrong**.

And trust me, they will go wrong. The sun will rise, the market will shift, and something will fail.

So here's the question:

When it breaks—do you hide? Or do you fix?

That's what people remember.

2. Salesperson Reputation – "Do I Trust You?"

This one's personal.

Every salesperson reading this—your name is your business card. Your reputation walks into the room before you do. And it lingers long after the pitch is done.

You can have the best product in the world, but if you show up as needy, arrogant, or slick—you're cooked.

People don't buy from salespeople.

They buy from **trusted experts**.

I once had a BMW guy I'd worked with for years. Honest, consistent, straight shooter. Over time, I bought *three* cars through him. Why? Because I trusted him. Not just the brand—*him*.

Then he left.

So I left too.

Ended up at Mercedes. Not because I suddenly hated BMW—but because the connection was *with him.*

That's what real salespeople don't understand. You're not just pitching a product.

You're pitching **yourself.**

When you're solid—when clients know you'll back them, fight for them, answer the phone when something breaks—that's what they remember. That's what they buy into.

Another personal story – I became a commission only sales rep for an organisation and my clients trusted me, sales were good and in year two I was paid a total of $363,000.00 in commissions.

The company decided to remove me and employ their own talent.

The result is sales halved in the next twelve months and 5 years later, the business has still not achieved the level of success they had when my reputation was at the forefront.

That's the power of reputation.

3. Business Reputation – "Will They Stand Behind It?"

This is the amplifier.

If the business is unreliable, disorganized, or inconsistent—it erodes even the best people and products.

This is what separates brands like Mercedes, Apple, and Rolex from everyone else.

It's *not* just the product. It's the consistency.

It's the **alignment between the promise and the follow-through.**

Let me give you a story.

I used to sell $100K elevating work platforms. Fantastic on paper. But two years in, we discovered a major flaw—cracks in the booms. Serious stuff. Lives-at-risk stuff.

The manufacturer?

Radio silence. Excuses. Deflection.

Eventually, they gave a token warranty. But it wasn't enough. So what did I do?

I took **$200,000 out of my own pocket** and made it right.

Not because I'm some hero. But because I understood something most businesses never do:

My reputation was worth more than my margin.

The clients knew. They saw what happened. And they kept buying from me—because I did the right thing.

The manufacturer?

Well, I changed suppliers, their market in Australia gone, millions in potential revenue wiped off.

Because they didn't protect their reputation. And I wouldn't let them damage mine.

I see this all the time, short term thinking and suppliers not standing behind their product.

The Power of the Three Reputations

Product	Salesperson	Business	Outcome
✅ Great	✅ Great	✅ Great	🔥 Sales fly. Brand equity grows. Clients return.
❌ Poor	✅ Great	✅ Great	⚠️ Short-term lift, long-term erosion.
✅ Great	❌ Poor	✅ Great	🧯 Client churn. Sales stagnate.
✅ Great	✅ Great	❌ Poor	💣 Salesperson leaves. Clients follow.
❌ Poor	❌ Poor	❌ Poor	🪦 Race to the bottom. Deep discounts.

You want to accelerate sales without burning cash, talent, or your own reputation?

Earn alignment across all three.

How Buyers Actually Think: The three brains

Now here's where this gets even more interesting.

Let's dive into the science. Because we're not just selling to buyers—we're selling to **brains**.

And those brains don't think the way you think they do.

According to the *three brain Model*, we have three layers:

1. **The Reptilian Brain** (the croc brain): primitive, reactive, survival-based

2. **The Limbic Brain** (mammalian brain): emotional, social, trust-based

3. **The Neocortex** (the human brain): logic, language, analysis

Let's break it down.

1. The Croc Brain – "Am I Safe?"

This is your gatekeeper. It's scanning for **threat**.

Anything that feels pushy, confusing, boring, needy—it rejects.

That's why traditional sales approaches don't work anymore. If your email looks like every other email, if your pitch feels too rehearsed, if your slide deck screams "template"—the croc brain shuts you down.

This is where **intrigue, curiosity,** and **simplicity** are your weapons.

Don't give the ending first. Don't frontload with benefits.

Set up. Intrigue. Reveal.

That's how you get through the gate.

Now let's talk reputation – If your reputation precedes you into any sales engagement, and the product reputation, salespersons reputation and companies reputation is already positive, the croc brain relaxes, it is not alert, meaning your pathway to the mammalian brain is clear and sales will rise accordingly.

2. The Mammalian Brain – "Do I Belong Here?"

This part of the brain is tribal. Emotional. Status-driven.

It's asking:

- Do I trust this person?
- Are they like me?
- Do they know what they're talking about?

And this is where **status** becomes everything.

If you enter the conversation from a place of neediness—if you're begging for the sale—you immediately lower your status.

High-status people don't chase. They qualify.

They say things like:

- "We may not be a good fit."
- "Let's see if it makes sense to work together."
- "Here's how we do things."

And buyers respect that.

It is how a salesperson protects and frames their reputation.

Because in the world of sales—**status equals trust**, trust = reputation

3. The Neocortex – "Let's Make a Decision"

Only once you've passed the first two do you get to this part.

This is where logic lives. Analysis. Price comparison. Terms and conditions.

But if you haven't earned the right to get here?

None of that matters.

The Power of Status in Sales

Let's take this deeper.

Most salespeople show up trying to **earn** trust by talking about themselves.

"I've been in the industry 20 years…"

"I work with companies just like yours…"

"I'm the leading provider of…"

Stop.

No one cares what *you* say about you.

They care what you **say about them.**

And here's where you flip the switch:

Start the conversation by **qualifying them.**

Ask yourself: are they worthy of *your* time?

Because when you flip the frame, you become the expert. The prize.

And when you're the prize—**they chase you.**

The Reputation Formula:

Darrell Hardidge states: customer excellence is the foundation of reputation.

He teaches that trust is built not by grand gestures—but by *consistent excellence.*

Think about it:

- A client asks for a follow-up and you deliver instantly— trust.

- A product breaks and you proactively solve it—trust.

- A team member owns a mistake before the client even notices—trust.

None of these are complicated.

But they're rare.

Why?

Because most companies optimize for **efficiency**, not **excellence**.

But here's the secret…

In a world of average service, consistency is your competitive advantage.

When All Three Reputations Align

So let's bring it home.

When the **product** is reliable,
the **salesperson** is trusted,
and the **business** follows through—

Magic happens.

No resistance. No haggling. No ghosting.

Clients stay. They refer. They return.

That's not luck. That's **reputation at scale**.

The Reputation Checklist

Here's your litmus test:

- ✅ Does your product deliver on its promises—even under pressure?

- ✅ Do your salespeople act with integrity—even when it costs them a deal?

- ✅ Does your business solve problems quickly—even if it wasn't your fault?

- ✅ Do you communicate clearly, follow through consistently, and lead with honesty?

If the answer isn't a confident "yes" to all four—start there.

Fix the cracks. Realign the mission. Rebuild trust.

Closing Thoughts:

Selling Is About Safety

We don't sell products.

We don't sell features.

We sell **certainty**.

Certainty that what you say will happen—will happen.

Certainty that if it doesn't, you'll make it right.

Certainty that if I buy from you—**I'm safe**.

And when you understand that?

Reputation becomes your most valuable asset.

It's not what you *say* about yourself.

It's what others *believe* when you're not in the room.

So go build it.

Protect it.

Be known for it.

Because in the end, **reputation isn't what you sell. It's what makes people buy.**

Martin Eade – The Sales Strategist

www.thesalesstrategist.com.au

CHAPTER 20

#1 MOST TRUSTED

CHAPTER 20
#1 MOST TRUSTED

The Final Measure of Leadership

In the end, there's only one question that really matters:

Are you the most trusted?

Not the biggest. Not the loudest.
Not the one with the slickest brand campaign or the latest tech stack.

The Most Trusted.

Because in every corner of your business—from culture to customer experience, supplier relationships to investor confidence—**trust is the multiplier, its leverage**. The defining metric that determines if your strategy is scalable, your people are loyal, your brand is respected, and your future is secure.

Trust Is Not Claimed. It's Earned.

You don't get to declare yourself or your company the most trusted. The market decides. Your people decide. Your partners decide.

And they decide based on **what they feel**, **what they see**, and **what they experience**—not what you say in a meeting or publish in a brand statement.

That's the essence of #1Reputation:
It's the pursuit of **authentic excellence**, where every interaction counts, every decision reflects your values, and every leader is aware of the **compounding effect** of consistent behaviour.

> *"The true purpose of business is to Add Value"*
>
> Buckminster Fuller

You Cannot Lead Without It

You can't lead a high-performing culture without being trusted. You can't drive customer loyalty without being trusted. You can't create investor confidence, supplier priority, or CX brilliance without it either.

And yet, most companies never measure it.

That's why the **#1Reputation framework** exists—to take what was once invisible and make it measurable, actionable, and scalable.

We created tools, audits, and language that allow your team to stop guessing and start knowing. Because what you don't measure, you can't improve. And what you don't improve eventually becomes your blind spot.

#1Reputation Is Culture in Motion

Let's recap what we've learned:

- Your **team reputation** is how your people show up when no one is watching. Are they aligned, empowered, and proud to represent the company?

- Your **customer reputation** is how the market experiences your value. Are they just satisfied, or are they loyal, appreciative advocates?

- Your **supplier reputation** is how your partners prioritise you. Do they give you their best—or just their leftovers?

- Your **owner and investor reputation** is how your stakeholders see your future. Do they believe you're building something worth betting on?

Your reputation is alive in every one of these relationships. And in each, you are either gaining trust—or losing it.

The Most Trusted Companies...

Through over **500,000 customer interviews**, we've identified the key traits of companies that hold the #1 spot in trust. They:

- Actively measure their reputation across all key segments

- Hold leadership accountable for behaviour, not just performance

- Train their teams not just to deliver service—but to appreciate the opportunity to serve

- Operate with a culture of responsibility—above the line thinking, every time

- Build predictive models to anticipate risk and act early

- Avoid assumptions. They replace internal opinions with data and customer truth

They don't rely on legacy, brand perception, or marketing spin. They **build the future** through clarity, intention, and follow-through.

The Final Distinction: Above the Line vs Below the Line

Let's not forget what ultimately defines greatness.

You've learned the power of the **Reputation Line**—the invisible divider between growth and decline.
Above the line: ownership, accountability, responsibility.
Below the line: blame, excuses, denial, and justification.

The companies that become #1 most trusted?
They **live above the line**. Especially when things go wrong.

They ask:

- *How did this happen?*

- *How can we improve?*

- *How do we support our people to act better next time?*

They teach this way of thinking across every level, from the front line to the boardroom. Because **culture isn't built on posters—it's built on behaviour**.

This Is Your Invitation

If you've come this far, you already know this matters. You're not chasing average. You're not after "good enough."

You're ready to build a legacy company.

So ask yourself now:

- Are you truly measuring your reputation—or guessing?

- Do you know where trust is leaking in your business?

- Are your people aligned behind a single standard of greatness?

- Have you empowered the team to own reputation at every level?

- What happens next—will you **act**, or will you assume?

Because here's the truth:

The most trusted companies don't assume. They audit.
They don't react. They lead.
They don't chase trust. They earn it, every day.

Closing thoughts:

If you want to be the most trusted, it's not about doing more. It's about doing what matters—on purpose, with integrity, consistently.

This book has given you the mindset, the questions, the metrics, and the roadmap. What you do with it now is the only thing that counts.

Because reputation isn't your logo. It's your legacy.

And legacies aren't built by chance.
They're built by choice.

Greatness awaits.

CHAPTER 21
YOUR REPUTATION IS THE ESSENCE OF YOU

#1

CHAPTER 21
YOUR REPUTATION IS THE ESSENCE OF YOU

Your reputation is the sum of all facets of your character.

It's the good and the bad, the strong and the weak, the wins and the learnings, the challenges overcome, the dreams fulfilled—and you're not done yet.

Over the years, I've had the privilege of working with some of the most extraordinary people. They're not always the loudest in the room. In fact, they're often the quiet ones—the steady hands who show up each day and give their best. They've built remarkable teams and businesses and have served their markets with unwavering integrity. They've earned their #**1R**—and it **precedes them** wherever they go.

Their greatest wealth lies not in possessions, but in **relationships**. They have built a deep reservoir of trust, so much so that with a single request, they can move mountains—not because of money, but because of **respect**.

I've also worked with incredible team members—people who treat their colleagues and customers like family. They are the invisible force behind every powerful brand. They build the culture. They drive the service. They are the heartbeat of companies with a #1R. If you're reading this, know **you can be this person**, if you choose to be.

Your greatest asset **is** your reputation. Build it like it's the **only one in the world**—because it is. Just like your DNA, your reputation is **uniquely coded**. And when you act with **integrity and intention**, the universe responds.

So, **who are you not to be the greatest version of yourself?** Who are you not to inspire others to be the same?

Be the one who sees possibility. Be the one who raises the standard. Be the one who turns values into action. Be the one who adds value, every step of the way.

Your reputation is your **identity**. It's your **voice**. And it's **always in motion**.

What path will you take it on? What doors will you walk through? What challenges will you rise to meet? What legacy do you want your reputation to leave behind?

Because **you are the only one** who truly knows what's possible for your life—until you make it real. You are also the only one who knows the limiting beliefs holding you back. So, choose. Choose the ones that serve you. Choose the version of yourself that creates the future you're proud of.

Never let anyone tell you what you cannot achieve. That voice usually comes from a lack of courage and fear—fear that doesn't belong to you. Only those with limited vision will try to limit yours. **They are not you**, and they do not see what you see. Stay clear. Stay focused.

Be the one who sees greatness in others—and in doing so, the world will begin to reflect that greatness back to you.

This is your time. This is your story. This is your reputation.

Lead with purpose. And build a legacy worthy of the name you carry.

Greatness Awaits

Live long and prosper.

Darrell

Darrell

Your Call to Action

The Courage to Ask the Hard Questions

You've just read through the insights, distinctions, principles, and strategies that define what it takes to build and protect a #1 Reputation. Not theory. Not fluff. The real, tested truths that separate average from extraordinary.

But now it's not about what you've read—
It's about what you do next.

"To know and not to do, is worse than not knowing at all"

Marshall Thurber

So, what will you do with what you now know?

This is your invitation to begin again—at a new level. To **look at your business, your leadership, your culture, and your market reputation through a sharper lens.** To ask the hard questions most avoid. To challenge the assumptions others accept. To think beyond the current objectives of customer experience and confront the truth of your reputation.

Start here:

- **Are we really as good as we think we are—or have we mistaken momentum for mastery?**

- **Do we actually know what our customers, our team, and our suppliers think of us—or are we guessing?**

- Are our internal beliefs and behaviours aligned with the reputation we claim to have—or is there a gap we haven't faced?

- Do we have the courage to measure what matters—or are we still relying on opinions and excuses?

- And most importantly… Who in our company is *truly* responsible for our reputation right now?

If these questions make you pause—**good.**
That's where leadership lives.
In the pause. In the reflection. In the inquiry.

This book was never meant to simply be read. It was written to be activated.
To challenge you. To provoke thought. To start conversations that matter.
The kind of conversations that shift culture, sharpen teams, deepen trust—and define legacies.

So now—start the audit.

Ask the questions.
Review your assumptions.
Call a meeting.
Have the uncomfortable conversations.
Pull the curtain back.
Take the lead.

Because the most powerful leaders are not those who always have the answers—
They're the ones brave enough to ask the questions no one else will.

Who in your team has the correct theory and the experience to measure your reputations? Even if you have a process for CX, stress test it and see how it stands up to the Reputation Index.

> *"What you don't measure you can't manage"*
>
> W. Edwards Deming

Measuring against excellence is the highest standard possible; just assuming you know is negligence.

> *"Sometimes it's what we know that isn't so"*
>
> Bill Allen

Building a #1 Most Trusted Reputation is never finished. It's not a destination—it's a discipline. What matters most is how you start, and how you continue.

So now that you know many of your company's beliefs about reputation may not be as certain as they seem—what will you do?

Will you make mis-take #1 and **Not Act When You Should Act,** will you think about it, and then eventually, like most, do nothing?

I've designed and delivered strategies for hundreds of reputation research projects, and no two have ever been the same. Nor should they be. Reputation cannot be managed with a cookie-cutter approach; it demands clarity, precision, and a strategy tailored to your culture, your customers, and your market.

Get in touch, and let's explore how we can help you master your most powerful asset—your reputation—and use it to elevate both your leadership and your business.

Your #1Reputation is not a label.
It's a standard. A choice. A responsibility.
Make it your mission. Act now.

Greatness Awaits

Author's final words

On a personal note:

Whether you're a CEO, a team leader, a key executive, or someone just starting your leadership journey—thank you for reading this book. I hope it challenged you. I hope it gave you a language for what you've felt but couldn't quite articulate. And I hope it becomes a catalyst for the kind of transformation that turns good companies into great ones—and respected businesses into #1R leaders.

The greatest risk is not what you don't know—it's what you assume. The **Great Assumption** has destroyed more businesses than poor products, weak strategies, or economic downturns combined. Assuming that reputation is "fine" because revenue is strong or complaints are low is the most dangerous game you can play as a leader.

So here's the challenge: **What will you do with what you now know?**

You can close this book, nod in agreement, and go back to business as usual. Or you can **ACT**—decisively and intentionally—on the strategies, audits, and distinctions you've just been given.

Because a #1 Reputation is never an accident.
It's never a checklist.
It's never a story you tell about yourself.

It is built every day by the **clarity of your leadership, the culture of your team, the trust of your customers, and the respect of your suppliers.**

I've shown you how to measure it, how to protect it, and how to leverage it into growth and margin. But the final responsibility is yours.

I'd love to hear your story, your questions, or where this work takes you next. You can connect with me and the team at:

- **www.1reputation.net**

- via LinkedIn or email through the website

And ask about how to bring **#1Reputation** strategy into your business, boardroom, or leadership offsite.

> *"You don't get to choose if you have a reputation. You only get to choose what it's known for."*
>
> *Darrell Hardidge*

About the Author

Darrell Hardidge has spent over two decades committed to one mission: service excellence that defines reputations—and builds powerful companies. As the founder of Saguity, a Melbourne-based consultancy, he's led the change in **measuring customer experience (CX)** at a level few can rival.

His company has conducted over **500,000 live interviews** with customers across Australia and internationally, ranging from billion-dollar national brands to local vets. Why? Because no matter what you do, it's how you do it that defines your reputation. That's the truth behind every success story.

Darrell isn't a theorist—he's a builder. He's designed **CX questionnaires, analytical frameworks, reporting systems, and growth strategies** that give leaders crystal clarity on what it takes to become #1 in their market. His IP doesn't measure the average standard of satisfaction—it uncovers **the hidden drivers of appreciation, loyalty, and advocacy** that define excellence.

He pioneered the model **Appreciation Certified**™, shifting the industry's obsession from basic satisfaction scores to meaningful emotional connection. He developed the **CX Due Diligence** model, used to protect multi-million dollar transactions by verifying goodwill and customer capital. His newest innovation, **The Reputation Index**™, is a complete redefinition of how reputation is measured and valued—moving well beyond generic NPS or C-Sat into **multi-layered, market-anchored trust metrics**.

This book marks Darrell's **third publication** in the CX field and brings the journey full circle: But this book is different. This one is about the **entire system of reputation**—from internal culture to external trust. From beliefs to behaviours. From theory to execution. From data to insight. It combines real-world data, leadership mindset, cultural structure, and measurable trust into one clear framework. As Darrell says often: *Clarity leads to power.* And this book gives you both.

Through Saguity, Darrell and his team have measured reputations and coached **some of the most influential companies in Australia**, creating cultures and structures that consistently outperform their competition—not by luck, but by strategy and clarity. His insights have shaped high-performing teams, and helped leaders take full ownership of their market reputation. His philosophy is simple but powerful:

"Great cultures don't happen by chance. They happen by intention, clarity, and accountability."

Greatness Awaits

Bonus Offer

Building your #1Reputation will take more than just reading this book. It will take specific targeted actions. To help get you in play I have the following bonus offers for you.

Bonus #1

- Once you've been online (www.1reputation.net) and completed your #1Reputation audit you can connect and we can discuss the appropriate strategy required from your results. 30 min consultation, valued at $495 but yours for free

Bonus #2

- If you would like to discuss any part of this book and the strategies to building a #1Reputation in your company we can explore how you can implement the process. 60 min consultation valued at $995 but yours for free

- Mention this book for a 10% discount on any reputation research, workshop or coaching program

Claim your free bonus offers now by going to

www.1reputation.net

#1REPUTATION
YOUR GREATEST ASSET

www.ingramcontent.com/pod-product-compliance
Lightning Source LLC
Chambersburg PA
CBHW071634200326
41519CB00012BA/2294